HOW TO
SURVIVE
ANYTHING

OUTDOOR LIFE

HOW TO
SURVIVE
ANYTHING

TIM MACWELCH
and the editors of
Outdoor Life

Illustrations by
TIM MCDONAGH
and Carl Wiens

weldon**owen**

CONTENTS

THE UNEXPECTED

THE UNPREDICTABLE

THE UNTHINKABLE

THE MATRIX

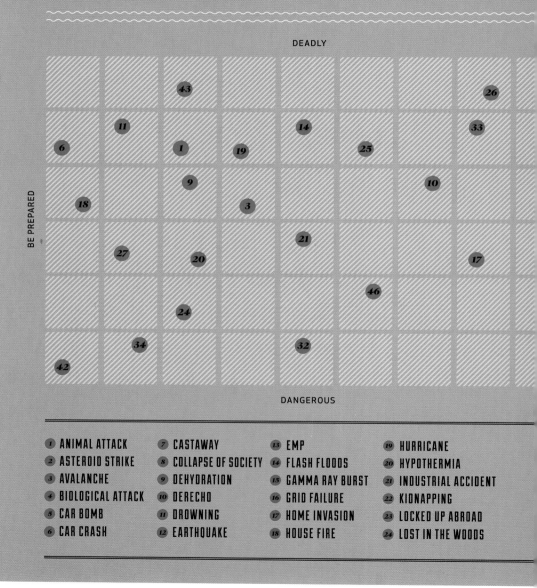

DEADLY

BE PREPARED

DANGEROUS

① ANIMAL ATTACK	⑦ CASTAWAY	⑬ EMP	⑲ HURRICANE
② ASTEROID STRIKE	⑧ COLLAPSE OF SOCIETY	⑭ FLASH FLOODS	⑳ HYPOTHERMIA
③ AVALANCHE	⑨ DEHYDRATION	⑮ GAMMA RAY BURST	㉑ INDUSTRIAL ACCIDENT
④ BIOLOGICAL ATTACK	⑩ DERECHO	⑯ GRID FAILURE	㉒ KIDNAPPING
⑤ CAR BOMB	⑪ DROWNING	⑰ HOME INVASION	㉓ LOCKED UP ABROAD
⑥ CAR CRASH	⑫ EARTHQUAKE	⑱ HOUSE FIRE	㉔ LOST IN THE WOODS

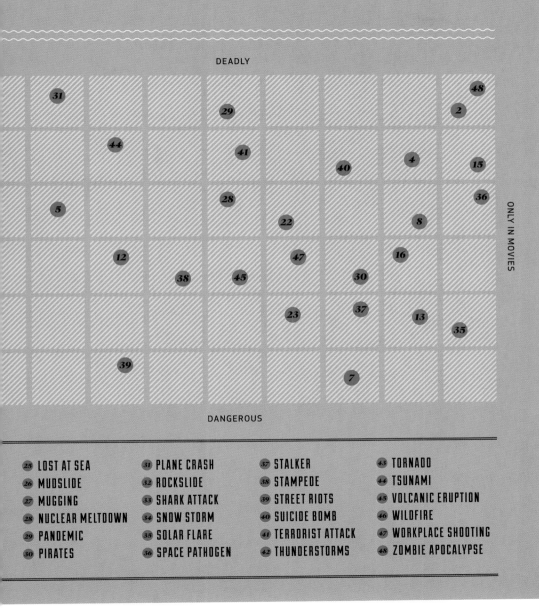

DEADLY

ONLY IN MOVIES

DANGEROUS

25	LOST AT SEA	31	PLANE CRASH	37	STALKER	43	TORNADO
26	MUDSLIDE	32	ROCKSLIDE	38	STAMPEDE	44	TSUNAMI
27	MUGGING	33	SHARK ATTACK	39	STREET RIOTS	45	VOLCANIC ERUPTION
28	NUCLEAR MELTDOWN	34	SNOW STORM	40	SUICIDE BOMB	46	WILDFIRE
29	PANDEMIC	35	SOLAR FLARE	41	TERRORIST ATTACK	47	WORKPLACE SHOOTING
30	PIRATES	36	SPACE PATHOGEN	42	THUNDERSTORMS	48	ZOMBIE APOCALYPSE

GOD FORBID!

One minute you're picking blueberries; the next you're being dragged into the brush by a grizzly. Or you're at 33,000 feet, choosing a beverage, when there's a sickening lurch, followed by screams and darkness. Or the new buddy you met is suddenly pulling you outside, and there's a car with its engine running, waiting for you. What do you do?

Every one of those scenarios seems almost extravagantly unlikely. Yet every year, people just like you encounter these very incidents, and how they survive says a lot about their mental and physical preparation. The point of this book is to start that process: to remind you that chaos is all around and to equip you with the skills required to be a survivor.

There's no better guide to this world of rife and ruin than Tim MacWelch. Tim is one of the nation's foremost authorities on survival. He teaches our most lethal soldiers how to live for weeks on mushrooms and moss. Dropped into the wilderness, Tim could walk out healthy and well-fed a year later, wearing a wolf hide and picking his teeth with a bear claw. Tim is the guy you want with you when your car goes off the road, the lights go out, or the chemical factory down the street starts to belch and fume.

But here's the thing: Tim's the nicest guy you'll ever meet. He's funny and smart, and likes to cuddle small animals. In other words, he's one of us. But he knows the worst can happen, so he's taught himself—and many others—the specific, sequential, often simple steps required to survive anything.

Tim's grounded, sensible advice is wrapped around the gorgeous illustrations by Tim McDonagh. You'll be tempted to gaze at this beautiful art as your ship goes down, terrorists storm the building, and the tornado alerts blare. But resist the urge to give in. Instead, fight, defend, combat, endure. Survive. It can be difficult, painful, and alarming. But it's far preferable to the alternative.

ANDREW MCKEAN
Editor-in-Chief, *Outdoor Life*

YOU CAN DO IT

I believe that if you're truly prepared, you can survive anything. This isn't about owning the latest survival kit, or sitting through a bunch of doomsday prep classes. It's about the skills, knowledge, and mindset that everyone should possess. This life-sustaining assortment includes keen situational awareness, a willingness to improvise and adapt, the knowledge of what basic survival supplies each household should keep, and the mental toughness to persevere when things get rough. The world can be a dangerous place, and we don't always see the danger coming. That's why you need to know how to react. At its core, survival is all about reacting correctly to the danger at hand. Make the right move, and you'll live to fight another day. But make the wrong move, and you'll be on the fast track to activating your life insurance policy—and if your demise is legendary enough, you'll receive a Darwin Award.

The survival situations described in this book range from the most likely issues you'll face in your lifetime to the things that you'll probably never see. This arrangement is intentional, and it mirrors a very critical teaching point: Deal with the biggest threat first. It's practically a mantra at my survival school, and its meaning is simple. Take care of the most pressing threat to your survival before you do anything else. This means that you'll have to figure out (rapidly and accurately) what would kill you the quickest, and remedy the problem effectively. Then take care of the next most likely threat, and so on. Do this until the immediate threats are eliminated, and your survival is very likely.

You can always get sucker-punched by bad luck, despite your best efforts, or you might wind up in a situation that isn't discussed in this book. But you'll adapt, whatever the case, and with the basics you'll learn here for handling a staggering variety of emergencies, you really can survive just about anything man or nature throws at you.

TIM MACWELCH

BE PREPARED

SURVIVAL IS ALL ABOUT BEING PREPARED AND MAKING THE RIGHT CHOICES. THIS PREPARATION SHOULD INVOLVE TRAINING, KNOWLEDGE, SKILLS, AND SUPPLIES, BECAUSE YOU'LL NEED THEM ALL. HERE ARE YOUR ABSOLUTE BASICS, THE FOUNDATIONAL SKILLS AND GEAR FOR SURVIVAL.

A big part of surviving in the moment lies in being prepared beforehand. To put it another way, if an ounce of prevention is worth a pound of cure, then an ounce of prep is worth a pound of survival. But what exactly should we prepare for?

Since doomsdays and getting lost in the wild are pretty rare events, it makes the most sense to prepare for the more likely events that could strike you and your family. Although crime prevention, natural disaster prep, and fire drills are a lot less exciting than zombie-apocalypse training, the former are a lot more likely to actually happen. Thankfully, a lot of the prep work for day-to-day emergencies is easy.

Talk about survival with your family, and have a plan for what to do if disaster strikes while you're separated. Now is the time—not during or after the emergency—to make plans detailing how you'll cope and where you'll meet up, especially if mom and dad are at work, Susie's in day care, and Bobby's at the high school. Basic, everyday survival skills aren't hard to perform, but they do require some effort. Make time to talk to your kids about the dangers that strangers pose, and how important it is to lock up. Familiarize your family with evacuation routes and alternate ways to get out of town in an emergency. Stock up on basic disaster supplies as detailed in this book. Add a few layers of security to your home, and do a fire drill twice annually when you change your smoke alarm batteries.

Teach your family members, especially the young ones, to stay put if they become lost on a hike or campout. When staying still, they are much easier to find. Have them wear a whistle and carry a long-life flashlight on their outdoor adventures. These two items will give them the tools to signal for help, and to stay calm if darkness falls before help arrives.

Generally speaking, this is easy stuff, and it can even be fun if you do it right. Make sure that all of your family members will make the right choices in the event of a problem, and you're likely to have no problems at all.

EVERYDAY CARRY ITEMS It's wise to have a set of everyday carry (EDC) items—survival essentials that can be carried in a pocket or purse and should always be kept on hand. These are separate from the bug-out gear and other survival packs you may have, but they play a supporting role for the larger kits. EDC gear is also your back-up plan, in the event you can't reach your larger assortments of gear.

CELL PHONE Ideally your phone includes some extras, such as a flashlight, compass feature, and a variety of survival apps.

KEY CHAIN Your key chain can be a catch-all of odds and ends. A spark rod, mini-flashlight, cordage, pepper spray, and any number of other survival items can live next to your keys at all times.

POCKET KNIFE A simple yet sturdy folding blade knife can perform a multitude of survival chores.

HANDGUN With the right permits, compact firearms can be carried in many areas, including a concealed carry weapon for self-defense in a secure holster.

FLASHLIGHT A flashlight serves a variety of needs, from obvious illumination to signaling and even defense (blinding your opponent). Make sure you have one (or more) handy, and always with charged batteries.

ALWAYS BE READY
As Philip K. Dick once said, just because you're paranoid doesn't mean they're not after you. In the same vein, when it comes to the kinds of survival situations we're discussing here, you could say that rational and appropriate levels of preparedness never hurt anybody.

While you don't want to live a life of dread, filled with fear and paranoia, you should always be prepared to go into survival mode at a moment's notice.

This kind of readiness can be accomplished by staying alert to the events around you, keeping on top of current news, having survival skills and gear at your disposal, planning for likely hazards (and some not-so-likely ones), and continually learning from books like this one, survival classes, and like-minded survival fans.

YOUR BUG-OUT BAG A BOB (bug-out bag) is a collection of goods that you would need to survive if you had to flee your home with no guarantee of shelter, food, or water during an emergency. Think of the BOB as your survival insurance policy for any disaster or mayhem. There may not be one perfect, universally agreed-upon set of equipment, but with a core set of items (similar to those used in backpacking) you can put together a BOB suited for a wide variety of situations. Most people use either a backpack or a duffle bag as the container for their goods, which should include basic survival essentials and a few irreplaceable items. Fill your BOB with a minimum of the following, with most items sealed in zip-top bags in order to prevent water damage:

SHELTER Shelter items may include a small tent and sleeping bag, or a tarp and blanket.

WATER A couple quarts or liters of drinking water, and purification equipment to disinfect more water.

FOOD High-calorie, no-cook foods like protein bars, peanut butter, trail mix, and other shelf-stable items.

FIRST AID First aid, sanitation, and hygiene supplies (see page 17).

FIRE Fire-starting methods.

COOKING A small pot for boiling water or cooking.

TOOLS A few basic tools: a knife, duct tape, rope, etc.

CLOTHES Extra clothes appropriate for the season.

LIGHT Flashlight with extra batteries.

CASH The world runs on it, usually.

FILES A digital backup of all your important documents. This could be a thumb drive with your bank info, insurance documents, wills, and family photos and videos.

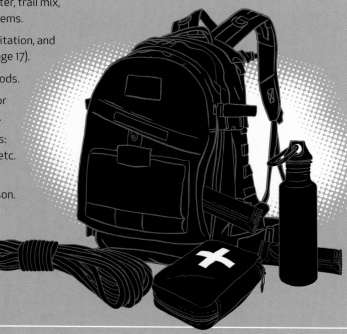

CAN'T DO WITHOUT

YOUR GET HOME BAG Your Get Home Bag is leaner and meaner than the average BOB, and its purpose is clear: getting you home. If you are using a Get Home Bag (GHB), you're planning on camping out in your own house, not in the woods or wherever you may find yourself when disaster strikes. If you're not sure what you'd need to get home in the event of an emergency, use this skeleton structure to get started and flesh it out to match your needs and concerns.

SECURITY Items like a large knife, pepper spray, or stun gun could be stashed in your GHB for personal defense.

SHELTER This could be simply a bare-bones tarp and fleece blanket, or a space blanket if storage room is limited.

WATER Buy 2 quarts (or liters) of bottled water, as they will keep for a while. Also get the Micropur tablets from Katadyn. Each tablet will disinfect one quart of water, so you can refill your bottles as needed.

FIRST AID This could be the standard camping first aid kit, which will work for either a GHB or BOB.

FOOD Remember, lean and mean is our slogan here. One Mainstay 2400 Emergency Food Ration will be about right for a GHB, or even a fistful of Snickers bars in a pinch, if you can keep them from melting.

OLD SUPPLIES An old pair of walking shoes or hiking boots are of key importance in this kit, as is a seasonally appropriate set of clothes and outerwear. Also consider a small roll of duct tape, a contractor trash bag, a head lamp with spare batteries, some cash in small bills, waterproof matches, a lighter, toilet paper, hand sanitizer, a compass, a local topography map, a multitool, some signaling gear, and one of your old cell phones—fully charged, but turned off (it can still dial 911).

ESSENTIAL GEAR

STOCK YOUR FIRST AID KIT Everyone should have a first aid kit at home and in their vehicle. Just think of this as the standard accessory for life. First aid is the most likely survival skill that you'll ever employ in your lifetime. You can perform it on yourself and on others who are in need. Start with this list of the basics, and don't be afraid to add to your kit as you see fit.

QuickClot sponge

Blood stopper dressing kit

Several additional dressings and bandages for smaller wounds

Several pairs of Nitrile gloves

Small EMT shears

Pack of 10 suture strips

Povidone-Iodine prep pads or alcohol pads

THE UNEXPECTED

Do you have the know-how to survive a home-leveling blaze or being caught outside in a blizzard? What would you do if you were lost in the wilderness or involved in an automobile accident? The events covered in this chapter are unusual, but they should not be unexpected—they are some of the most likely survival scenarios that you might face over your lifetime. And these are the types of calamities that you should have seen coming, particularly if you live and work in harm's way. One man's "very unlikely" survival emergency is another man's "every Thursday." For instance, in a developing nation, the electrical grid may go down all the time. In New York City, it's a rare and terrifying event. The pages that follow walk you through the right and wrong choices to make as you react to these common calamities.

ANIMAL ATTACKS

PINNED DOWN BY A RAVENING GRIZZLY. STALKED BY A HUNGRY MOUNTAIN LION. CHASED DOWN A DARK ALLEY BY A PACK OF VICIOUS DOGS. THESE ARE THE THINGS THAT EVOKE A PURE, PRIMAL TERROR, A FEAR THAT HITS US RIGHT IN OUR STONE-AGE BRAINS. AND HERE'S HOW TO SURVIVE THEM.

*T*hrilling tales of survival often start with a dangerous animal encounter. Any story that begins, "There I was, face to face with the biggest grizzly I'd ever seen" is going to get your audience right where they live. And with good reason. The fear of dying by animal attack is as old as woolly mammoths and saber-toothed tigers.

This primal fear resurfaces when we square off against contemporary predators. With today's dangerous animals, there's a lot of overlap in what you'd do to survive: make yourself as big as possible, make noise, avoid eye contact, and back away slowly. But these tricks don't work on all beasts. Opening your coat to look bigger won't help you with a protective mama bear or a hungry gator. For the maternal bear, a bigger you means an even bigger threat to the cub. And to the alligator, you just got a lot meatier looking. You need the right techniques to use on each predator. In the pages that follow, we'll break those techniques down, animal by animal.

BE ANIMAL AWARE Animals are everywhere. Yes, I realize that seems too obvious to even mention. But what I mean here is that animal attacks can happen at any time and in any place. Of course any sensible person will be cautious when hiking a remote trail or camping in the woods, but your guard may drop in that campground's parking lot, or when strolling down a suburban street. When such an unexpected encounter happens, the odds aren't in your favor, friend. More people face down bears in seemingly safe campgrounds (or their own backyards) than deep in the wild. And dog attacks can happen anywhere. Keep your head on a swivel, as they say in the military, and use your situational awareness skills to stay alert to potential furry, fanged hazards everywhere you go.

THE STATS

2,132 POUNDS (967 KG) Top weight ever recorded for a grizzly.

902 POUNDS (409 KG) Record weight of the heaviest known black bear.

700 PSI (48 BAR) Bite force of a black bear's jaws.

35 MPH (56 KPH) Top speed of a running or sprinting black bear.

10 FEET (3 M) Height of a big grizzly on its hind legs.

800,000 Dog bites requiring medical care in the U.S. every year.

THE MATRIX

DEADLY

BE PREPARED

ONLY IN MOVIES

DANGEROUS

1. Grizzly Bears
2. Black Bears
3. Mountain Lions
4. Wild Dogs
5. Urban Attack Dogs
6. Wolves
7. Alligators

GRIZZLY BEARS These huge beasts can typically weigh up to 800 pounds (360 kg) and stand 7 feet (more than 2 m) tall on their hind legs. The true danger with grizzlies arises if you surprise one, or encounter a mother and cub. Do not run, as that action will likely trigger a predatory attack (like a cat going after a scurrying mouse). Instead, back away slowly. If the huge bruin charges you, your best bet is to curl up tightly on the ground and play dead. How to tell if you're facing a grizzly? Besides the size, they have brown fur and a distinctive hump at their shoulders.

BLACK BEARS While they're smaller and seem less scary, statistically, black bears are more predatory against humans than grizzlies. If you find that one of these bears has come into camp, don't run. Instead, prepare to fight for your life. Face the bear and make yourself appear larger by waving your arms high. Shout at the top of your lungs. Fire a few warning shots into the ground, if you have a firearm. Be ready to actually shoot the bear if it continues to advance. If you're without a gun, be ready to fight for your life with sticks, rocks, a knife, or whatever's handy.

MOUNTAIN LIONS Mountain lions are big cats, not too different in habits and diet from other big cats like lions and tigers. Also known as cougars or pumas, these lions are ambush predators, and favor attacking from high vantage points. They are also excited by fast-moving prey, which is likely the reason that trail runners and mountain bike riders are occasionally singled out. Be extra alert when traveling through areas with a cougar population and rock outcrops they can jump down from. Should you get on the radar of one of these skilled predators, try to look bigger and fight as you would against a black bear.

WILD DOGS Feral dogs are typically medium-size critters of 30 to 40 pounds (13 to 18 kg), and can be a blend of almost any breed. Some wild dogs are simply stray house pets, while others were born in the wild and are truly feral. Though wild dogs rarely kill people in actual attacks, their high incidence of rabies makes them very dangerous. More

ANIMALS CAN SMELL YOUR FEAR

FALSE It is true that many animals have a far, far more developed sense of smell than humans. A bloodhound, for example, can follow a person's trail just by the microscopic flakes of dead skin on the ground. And a bear may be able to find you from the scent of the granola in your backpack. Bears have been documented to smell food from over 35 miles (56 km) away. But your pheromones? Most studies suggest that animals can only smell these subtle chemical cues within their own species. That said, it is true that animals may be good at picking up other cues, such as your body stance, nervous fidgeting, and eye contact.

than 55,000 people die from rabies each year, and dogs are the primary source. They are silent stalkers and pack hunters; you may not know they are on your trail until too late. Since a dog pack can outrun and outfight an unarmed human, your best bet is to shimmy up the nearest tree.

URBAN ATTACK DOGS Numerous breeds of dogs are raised to be "attack" or "guard" dogs. Sadly, some are even bred as fighting dogs. When these become strays, the resulting dog can become a threatening scavenger on the fringes of urban and suburban areas. Fight or climb (maybe jump on the roof of a car, a dumpster, or a high wall) to get away from these canines, but don't run. You'll just give them the chase they were hoping to get.

WOLVES The gray wolf (aka the timber or western wolf) is the largest wild canine in the Northern Hemisphere—large males can weigh 95 to 99 pounds (43 to 45 kg). Wolves favor

BEING CHASED BY A BEAR? DROP THE WEIGHT— AND SOME BAIT. YOUR FOOD- LADEN BACKPACK MAY DISTRACT THE BEAST, AND THE LIGHTER LOAD HELPS YOU, TOO. WHILE THE ANIMAL IS DEVOURING YOUR BROWN BAG LUNCH, RUN FOR SAFETY.

CAN'T DO WITHOUT

BEAR SPRAY If there was ever a magic bullet for predators (besides bullets), it's bear spray. This is a great item for bear country, and it works on other critters, too (including humans). For maximum effectiveness, check that the spray is EPA registered, sprays over 25 feet (7.5 m), and has an orange colorant. The color is believed to be the biggest deterrent. Bears are smart and instinctively afraid of new things. They are not accustomed to an orange stinging cloud and loud hiss. They will run off, then look back, trying to figure out what just happened. While they're moving, you should be running the other way.

remote wilderness areas and hunt in packs, but wolf attacks are very rare outside of Europe and Asia. Wolves can carry rabies, and rabid wolves are often much more aggressive than rabid dogs (in one study, rabid wolves were 15 times more aggressive). If threatened, climb the closest tree, and be prepared to live up there until the wolves move on or rescue arrives.

ALLIGATORS Swamp- and wetland–loving creatures of the American southeast, large male alligators can grow to lengths of 14 feet (4.3 m) and weigh over 990 pounds (450 kg). These animals are generally timid around humans, but nesting females can become aggressive if they feel their nest is threatened. Alligators that have been fed by humans also lose their natural fear and begin to associate people with mealtime. They can become dangerous, and for this reason, feeding wild alligators is illegal. If a gator charges you, run in a zigzag pattern until you've outdistanced it.

A Grizzly Tale of Terror

When Dr. John Wuskie set off on a guided elk hunt, he was hoping for the adventure of a lifetime—not a struggle for his life. About an hour into their stalk, his guide, Pete Clark, dropped into a crouch—he'd spotted an elk. Wuskie hunched, squinting in the direction Clark was looking, to see a massive bull bedded on the ridge.

As Wuskie aimed his Remington .30/06, he suddenly had the urge to look over his shoulder. There he saw a female grizzly, followed by two cubs, trotting along the ridge 20 yards (18 m) to his right. He hoped they'd pass by without seeing him, but as the sow turned, she spotted Wuskie and charged instantly, before he could raise his rifle and aim properly. He got off a wild shot, but she just kept coming.

The bear landed on him with incredible force, "Like being shot out of a cannon," he recalls. Clark, who usually didn't carry a loaded gun while guiding, fumbled with loading his Remington 700 7mm. As he frantically loaded, the bear sank her teeth deep into Wuskie's flailing arm. Drawing on his long-ago wrestling training, Wuskie managed to flip face down, and the bear sunk her teeth into his back. Wuskie was sure he would die there, and Clark was unable to get off a shot for fear of also shooting Wuskie. He approached, trying to get a better angle, and the bear suddenly leapt up and ran away.

Wuskie's medical training allowed him to assess that his injuries were not life-threatening. Clark went to retrieve Wuskie's gun and to his amazement, the elk was still standing almost exactly where they'd seen it. He scrambled back down to tell Wuskie, asking, "Do you think you can shoot?"

Weak and losing blood, Wuskie managed to make the shot. Clark speed-dressed the big bull, and they made their way back to camp. Wuskie survived with some impressive scars, an amazing story, and a 5 by 6 rack on his wall at home.

HEAVY WEATHER

THE HURRICANE'S TORRENTIAL RAINS AND HOWLING WINDS REMIND US THAT WE ARE NOT IN CHARGE OF THIS WORLD. ONCE THE STORM'S FURY DWINDLES, THE FLOOD RISES. CHURNING WATER THREATENS EVERYTHING THAT THE WIND FAILED TO RIP FROM OUR GRASP. WHAT CAN YOU DO TO PREVAIL?

The weather can seem like our best friend—when it doesn't rain on the parade, or when our newly planted crops get a gentle measure of rainfall. But the forces that move air, moisture, and heat aren't always so loving and benevolent.

Nature's most violent storms can cause levels of destruction that leave your home, neighborhood, and community looking like a wasteland—or a battlefield. Every year, thunderstorms, hurricanes, flooding, mudslides, and hailstorms take their toll on the face of the earth, leaving devastation and ruin in their wake. Wind, water, mud, lightning, and hail can kill; but they do not do so without warning.

As the storm clouds gather, we have time to prepare. The radio, the television, and even our phones can signal impending danger. Will we join the masses who run out to the store for last-minute supplies of milk, bread, and toilet paper? Or will we hunker down with the carefully chosen supplies we have already stocked? Are we as ready as we think we are? You can be. Do it now.

AN ATTIC BECOMES AN ESCAPE In flood-prone areas, the attic space of your home can become the most important room in the house. Rather than storing your vital food, supplies, water, and gear at ground level (or worse, in a basement), you can create an "ark" out of that creepy, dusty attic. Following the ark theme a little further, you should keep an inflatable raft in the attic to act as a floating storage shelf or mode of exodus. Have an axe up there, too—or, better yet, a chainsaw. Now you can cut your way out and make an aquatic escape. Remember to cut only a few trusses, to keep the roof from falling in. Wear safety glasses to keep sawdust and shingle grit out of your eyes. And hope the ghosts up there don't know how to use a chainsaw.

THE STATS

90 Average number of Americans killed each year by storm-related flooding.

27,501 Number of people killed in the deadliest hurricane on record, in the Caribbean in 1780.

8 INCHES (20.3 CM) Diameter of the largest verified hailstone.

$81 BILLION Hurricane Katrina's damage costs.

1 IN 12,000 Your odds of being struck by lightning.

71.9 INCHES (183 CM) Highest recorded rainfall, on Réunion Island in 1969.

THE MATRIX

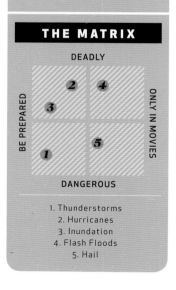

DEADLY

BE PREPARED

ONLY IN MOVIES

DANGEROUS

1. Thunderstorms
2. Hurricanes
3. Inundation
4. Flash Floods
5. Hail

THUNDERSTORMS A nice rainfall can be refreshing, but it can quickly turn deadly. Thunderstorms may be small compared to hurricanes, but they still carry significant destructive force and average 15 miles (24 km) in diameter.

All thunderstorms are dangerous, as they produce deadly lightning and often high winds and hail. There are approximately 100,000 thunderstorms each year in the United States, roughly 10 percent of which are classified as "severe" by the National Weather Service—meaning they boast damaging winds of at least 58 mph (93 kph) or hail at least ¾ inches (19 mm) in diameter.

To be safe, you should always seek shelter before a thunderstorm hits, so if you hear the rumbling, go indoors. Fully enclosed buildings offer the best protection. Their electrical wiring and metal piping offer a grounding effect in the event of a lightning strike. And of course, the building itself provides shelter from the wind and blowing debris. During the storm, just stay away from conductive things like wiring, corded telephones, and plumbing pipes and fixtures. Continue to avoid these items for 30 minutes after the storm, in case of lingering lightning.

HURRICANES A hurricane is a large tropical storm with a maximum sustained wind speed of 74 mph (119 kph) or greater. The most important things you can do if a hurricane threatens your area are to prepare your home, business, yard, and vehicles—and stay alert to the watches, warnings, and advisories in your region.

When advised, shutter or board up your windows, and bring in any outdoor furniture, toys, garbage cans, bird feeders, and the like, as they can become missiles. Prep your vehicles with a full tank of gas and basic emergency supplies (a first aid kit, food, water, tools, and jumper cables).

Be ready to hunker down, or to evacuate with your family and pets, should your area receive evacuation orders. Many deaths occur because people think they understand their area's weather patterns and ignore orders to evacuate, or because they waited until the last minute. The fact is, you may well know your local storm history—until that once-in-a-lifetime Katrina or Sandy comes along. Don't risk it.

CAN'T DO WITHOUT

SANDBAGS Properly stacked, as shown below, sandbags are a very effective way to hold back rising waters. Store empty burlap sacks or specially manufactured plastic ones in an accessible place. When the waters start to rise, fill them with (you guessed it!) sand, ideally, but heavy soil will do in a pinch. Don't tie the bags off, just stack in tightly overlapping layers, as shown. Filling the bags is a two-person job—one holds the bag open while the other shovels sand to fill no more than halfway full.

FLOODS Inundation can occur slowly and predictably due to known rainfall or snowmelt, or it can happen in the blink of an eye as a violent and unforeseen flash flood. Floods normally take more than 6 hours to occur. Flash floods, on the other hand, can happen in a much shorter period, due to heavy rainfall, dam or levee failure, or the sudden release of water from an ice-jammed river.

More than half of the life and property losses occur when vehicles are driven into dangerous flood waters, especially at night when visibility is hampered. Just 2 feet (0.6 m) of fast-moving water can sweep away most vehicles, even SUVs and trucks. And forget about trying to wade through. It only takes 6 inches (15 cm) of rushing water to knock you down and sweep you away. The best ways to deal with flooding are to evacuate before an event or to shelter in place. Never try to drive through flood waters. Turn around and find another way, or find high ground and stay put.

T / F

A CAR WILL INSULATE YOU FROM LIGHTNING

FALSE We've all heard that a vehicle's rubber tires will protect the occupants from lightning, as long as you're not touching metal parts inside the vehicle. This is not true. Electrocution can occur inside any vehicle that has been struck. Lightning causes 55 to 60 deaths and 400 injuries each year in the United States. And it accompanies every single thunderstorm. Sure, you are safer in a vehicle than out in the open or up in a tree (please don't climb a tree!), but you'll be *much* safer if you can get indoors. If you get caught without a car or shelter, lie flat on the ground in a low area to reduce your risk of lightning strike.

The Great Galveston Storm

While Katrina was the costliest hurricane ever to hit America, it was not the deadliest. That record belongs to a monster of a storm that hit Galveston, Texas in 1900, killing more people than any other weather event in the history of the U.S.

The booming, prosperous island city had weathered many storms since its founding in the 1800s, so news of another one approaching raised little concern. They were utterly unprepared for the winds—estimated as high as 145 mph (126 knots)—that ripped through the region, leaving almost inconceivable devastation in their wake.

In addition, the 15-foot (4.6 m) storm surge covered the entire island (the highest point at the time being only 8.7 feet [2.7 m] above sea level). Barometric pressure dropped so low that observers thought their equipment was malfunctioning.

Wooden buildings were knocked off of their foundations by the wind, and splintered by the surf. When the storm finally passed, over 8,000 people were dead (some estimates go as high as 12,000). Authorities passed out whiskey to help sustain the morale of those tasked with retrieving the bodies. The city was rebuilt, and once again thrives today.

HAILSTORMS Thunderstorms that drop frozen rain, aka hail, are often called hailstorms. Pellets of hail form when strong currents of air (called updrafts) carry water droplets to a height where they freeze. When the hail "stones" gather more moisture and grow too big to be supported by the updraft, they fall to the ground at speeds up to 100 mph (161 kph). Hail tends to do more damage to property than to people, though deadly freak hailstorms have occurred throughout history. On a day that became known as "Black Monday" in 1360, a hailstorm killed approximately 1,000 English soldiers near Paris during the Hundred Years' War. And in the 9th century, near the town of Roopkund, India, several hundred pilgrims were killed by a massive hailstorm. Dealing with hail is easy: seek shelter during thunderstorms, and you'll be sheltered from the hail as well.

CAN'T DO WITHOUT

ESSENTIAL GEAR Staying on top of current events can be vital to your family's safety. A simple weather radio can provide lifesaving information, such as evacuation orders, shelter instructions, and other critical directions. Make sure your radio has all the tools you'll need.

AM/FM RADIO For all local advisories.

WEATHERBAND SETTINGS Weatherband settings will allow you to pick up your local signal from the NOAA (National Oceanic and Atmospheric Administration) or the equivalent national information service.

BATTERIES Battery-operated options allow for portability.

ALTERNATE POWER SOURCES A hand crank or solar panel will keep working long after the power outage.

WATERPROOFING Your radio should be water resistant or waterproof.

ON THE WATERFRONT

DEADLY CURRENTS PULL YOU DOWN INTO THE DARKNESS. YOUR LUNGS BURN FROM HOLDING THEIR LAST BREATH. HUMANS NEED WATER TO LIVE, BUT THAT SAME FLUID CAN ALSO MEAN CERTAIN DEATH. WATER IS ALMOST EVERYWHERE, AND POSES AN EVER-PRESENT THREAT. BE PREPARED.

Some of our darkest fears and strongest nightmares involve water—dark, murky, hungry water that tries to swallow us whole. In particular, these fears revolve around the idea that water can take our lives. But death by water doesn't always happen in the ways that you'd expect.

It doesn't always involve swimming out too far and slipping quietly below the waves. A fall into icy waters can cause the simplest reaction—a gasp!—which can mean the end if you inhale just a few ounces of water. Intense currents can pound your body against rocks and piers, aggressively expelling the breath from your lungs—or dragging you out to be lost at sea. Even the warmest, calmest ocean waters can slowly and stealthily steal the heat from our bodies, leading to death from hypothermia—not drowning.

While millions of people work and play around water every day, the danger is still there. It's in our very nature to be drawn to the water, but sadly, sometimes it's the same lure as a moth to flame.

SPOT A DROWNING VICTIM Forget everything that Hollywood has taught you about drowning. A person in danger of drowning rarely screams, shouts, waves their arms, or splashes wildly. A real near-drowning victim has a very different look, and typically doesn't make a peep. Quite often, the person in distress has an involuntary reaction known as the "instinctive drowning response."

This quiet yet desperate reaction can be spotted if you know what to look for: a head that is low in the water, arms extended sideways and moving as if they were trying to lift the body out of the water, a lack of kicking or leg movement, and rapid breathing or "panting." These actions are usually performed silently and often go unnoticed by the average person.

THE STATS

88% Proportion of drowning victims who were not wearing life vests.

80% Proportion of victims who are male.

3,500 Number of annual drowning deaths in the U.S.

100 Number of people killed by rip currents at U.S. beaches each year.

15 MINUTES Average time before exhaustion or unconsciousness in freezing water.

2 TO 5 MINUTES Time it takes the venom of the Australian box jellyfish to kill a human.

THE MATRIX

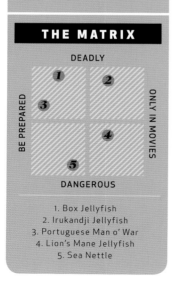

DEADLY

BE PREPARED

ONLY IN MOVIES

DANGEROUS

1. Box Jellyfish
2. Irukandji Jellyfish
3. Portuguese Man o' War
4. Lion's Mane Jellyfish
5. Sea Nettle

RIP CURRENTS Also called rip tides, these merciless currents can take swimmers by surprise, and are the leading surf hazard for beachgoers. Over three-quarters of lifeguard rescues are due to rip currents, and more than 100 people a year die in the U.S. from rip current–related drowning, more fatalities than are caused by lightning, tornadoes, and shark attacks combined. You can spot a rip current by looking for a choppy channel of water with a churning motion, a line of sea foam and debris that is moving out to sea, and a disrupted pattern of incoming waves. If you get caught in a current, the top priority is to avoid panic. If you keep calm and don't try to fight the rip current, you can swim sideways and parallel to the beach. Swimming in this direction will get you out of the rip current. Once free, swim away from the rip current at an angle and make your way toward shore.

DROWNING Water can kill, and it doesn't take much water to do the trick. If you find yourself in danger of drowning, the most important thing you can do is to keep calm. A panicked state makes you more of a hazard to yourself, and to anyone who might be trying to rescue you. Secondly, try to improvise some flotation. Flop wet clothing out of the water, and back down into it, to trap pockets of air to keep you afloat. If you are near a person you suspect might be drowning, ask them if they are all right. An actual answer will mean that they are fine, or at least still in control of their mental faculties. If you get no answer besides a vacant stare, they need help immediately. Try to get them to safety ASAP, and be aware that they may try to climb on top of you to get out of the water, endangering you both.

HYPOTHERMIA Water is an excellent conductor of heat, and as such, it is the perfect natural element to strip us of our warmth. It's actually possible to die from hypothermia in 80°F (27°C) water, it just takes a painfully long time to do so (about one week). On the flip side, hypothermia can happen in mere minutes when a person is immersed in water that's near freezing temperature. If you land in a water survival scenario, and have a PFD (personal flotation device), then you can assume a posture that lessens your heat loss. Cross

SKILL

SURVIVAL FLOAT When stranded in open water without a flotation device, you need to preserve your energy while waiting for rescue. The natural impulse is to float on your back, but in fact it's safer to float face down, arms and legs relaxed, raising your head only to take breaths. To breathe, lift your chin off your chest and pull your arms downward toward your body, and kick your legs if necessary. Breathe out, take a deep breath in, and go back to floating.

your feet and bend your knees. Fold your arms, with your hands under your armpits. "Curl up as best you can, while relying on the PFD to keep you afloat.

JELLYFISH STINGS Jellyfish can be a lot more hazardous than their goopy, gelatinous forms would suggest. For a creature with no brain that both eats and defecates with the same orifice, it has a stunningly complicated and effective weapon system. Most jellyfish have tentacles loaded with nematocysts. These stinging cells are triggered by touch, and build up intense internal pressures. When the nematocyst bursts, it fires out a harpoon laden with potent poisons. Not all jellyfish sting, but of those that do, some can be deadly within minutes. The average jellyfish sting, though painful, is not fatal. And despite what your 5th-grade buddies told you, peeing on it doesn't help. The best option is to get out of the ocean and wash the area with salt water. Salt water will deactivate the stinging cells while fresh water, tap water, or urine can reactivate the toxins in the stingers.

T/F

DROWN IN ICY WATER, AND YOU CAN COME BACK TO LIFE

TRUE Stranger than fiction, it's the case that intensely cold water can place a drowning victim into "suspended animation," preventing brain damage and reducing the body's need for oxygen. The heartbeat slows, respiration stops, and blood is routed to the vital organs (the heart, lungs, and brain). The current record for near-drowning under these conditions is 80 minutes, and stories of briefer submersions are plentiful. In cold water drowning, the victim should never be considered dead until the body has been rewarmed and is still unresponsive to resuscitation.

HELL ON WHEELS

CUBES OF BROKEN WINDSHIELD GLASS PELT THE DASHBOARD AS THE VEHICLE ROLLS. A NAUSEATING FEELING GRIPS YOUR STOMACH AS GRAVITY PULLS IT IN THE WRONG DIRECTION. THE WORLD LOOKS UPSIDE DOWN. STINGING SMOKE BEGINS TO BILLOW. THERE'S ONLY ONE WAY OUT.

C ars. We can't live without them (or so most of us believe), but we're also killed or injured by them at a shockingly high rate. Well over a million people worldwide are killed in car accidents each year, and as many as 50 million are injured—and experts believe that number will keep going up dramatically unless major changes are made in how and what we drive.

A wide range of catastrophes can happen in our cars, often in the blink of an eye. A broken brake line on a mountain road or an automotive splashdown in deep water could mean the end of the road. And more likely still, a collision with another vehicle or object can deliver the same impact as an explosion. Thankfully, there are ways to be safer on the roads and techniques that can save you in an accident.

While there are no guaranteed techniques that will ensure you survive all crashes or other terrifying four-wheeled incidents, the following hints should help you pull out of danger, and live to swerve (carefully!) another day.

SURVIVE A CRASH The oft-heard command to "brace for impact!" might work if your ship's about to hit an iceberg, but it's definitely not what you want to do in the seconds before a car crash. Unfortunately, a body with tensed muscles and locked joints will suffer more broken bones and trauma upon impact. Instead, take a lesson from those sleeping (or even intoxicated) passengers who, counter to what one would expect, can sometimes walk away from crashes without a scratch. Don't lock your arms, legs, or other joints. Just keep your hands at 8 o'clock and 2 o'clock on the steering wheel, to keep them out of the way of an airbag deployment, and try to stay loose so your body can bend and move with the impact.

THE STATS

30,000 Annual number of car-crash–related fatalities in the U.S.

50% Reduction in risk of injury or fatality if wearing a seat belt in a crash.

0.75 SECONDS Reaction time of the average motorist—enough to travel one car length per 10 mph (16 kph).

495°F (257°C) Ignition temperature of gasoline.

1 MINUTE Average time it takes for an automobile to sink in water.

THE MATRIX

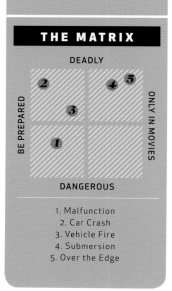

DEADLY

BE PREPARED

ONLY IN MOVIES

DANGEROUS

1. Malfunction
2. Car Crash
3. Vehicle Fire
4. Submersion
5. Over the Edge

MAJOR MALFUNCTIONS This sort of vehicular nightmare can take a variety of forms. A tire blows out, the gas pedal sticks, the brakes fail—any one of these mechanical failures can send your sweet ride careening out of control.

The solution for each of these failures involves two constants and one variable. The constants are that you STAY CALM and hit your hazard flashers. This is a tall order for a white-knuckle crisis situation, but staying calm will keep you thinking on your feet and the hazard flashers will warn nearby motorists that you are having a problem.

Now for the variables. If a tire blows violently, don't jerk the steering wheel. Maintain course and decrease speed gradually, while looking for a spot to pull off the road. If the gas pedal sticks, take the vehicle out of gear or turn off the engine. Then use your brakes to coast to a stop. If the brakes fail, downshift immediately, then use the emergency brake (parking brake). Depress the pedal or pull the lever as hard as you can. Give it a few seconds, and if the speed isn't decreasing, then look for a "soft" place to ditch the vehicle.

CAR CRASHES Motor vehicle crashes are a leading cause of injury and death by unnatural causes in the United States. Over 2.5 million drivers and passengers are treated in hospital emergency rooms each year as the result of being injured in motor vehicle collisions.

The primary lifesaver in vehicle collisions is wearing your seat belt. You've heard it a million times, but that's because it's true. The seat belt will prevent your body from being tossed about the cabin, thrown into the steering wheel, or ejected from the vehicle. Seat belts reduce injuries and death by 50 percent. Driving the speed limit is another major factor in crash survival. The faster the car is moving, the greater the kinetic energy will be. This force transfers from the vehicle to your body in the form of G-forces, which can result in injury or death. Driving a safer make and model of vehicle can also play a significant role in reducing the damage to passengers in an accident. And finally, stowing groceries and other loose items in the trunk means there's nothing in the car to go violently airborne and strike you in the event of a crash.

CAN'T DO WITHOUT

CAR ESCAPE TOOL An escape tool might be the most important thing in your car, especially if the seat belts won't release or the windows won't lower. There are many styles of auto safety tool on the market. Some clip onto seat belts so they are always within reach. Others have many features and resemble pocketknives or hammers. Whichever tool you choose, make sure you can access it quickly and easily, and that it can cut seat belts and break glass—at a minimum.

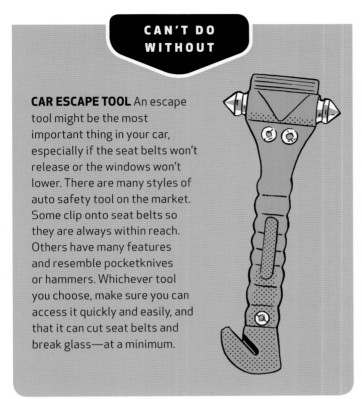

VEHICLE FIRES Any normal car has at least five potentially flammable fluids circulating in it at all times—gasoline, of course, but also motor oil, brake fluid, power steering fluid, and even coolant. Given this, it's surprising that vehicle fires don't happen more often.

Vehicle fires can accompany car crashes, or they can happen spontaneously. If the vehicle catches fire as the result of a collision, run, walk, or crawl away from it. It may not explode in the giant fireball you see in action flicks, but all the plastic components and petroleum-based liquids are flammable and the heat can be intense. The car *could* also blow up. And if you're tooling down the highway and begin to smell smoke (or worse, see flames and smoke from your vehicle), hit your hazard flashers and pull off the road as fast as you can. Get away from the car if you can safely and call 911 for the fire department.

IN WINTER, ADD SOME SMALL CANDLES TO YOUR CAR SURVIVAL KIT. IN AN ENCLOSED SPACE, CANDLES CAN GIVE OFF A SURPRISING AMOUNT OF HEAT, ALLOWING YOU TO SAVE THE CAR'S BATTERY. THEY ALSO MAKE YOU MORE VISIBLE TO RESCUERS.

A New Year's Miracle

It was New Year's Eve 2011 when Roger Andersen set out with two of his kids and a 9-year-old neighbor for a ski trip in Utah's Bear River mountains. The drive involves 30 miles (48 km) of sharp turns and switchbacks, but Andersen wasn't worried—the 46-year-old local had made the drive many times before in icy conditions. Little did he realize how different this day would be.

Rounding a hairpin turn, Andersen saw a van that had spun out on the icy road, presenting a driving hazard. He tapped his brakes, and the next thing he knew his car was sliding off the road and down an embankment, into the Logan River. The car rolled upon impact and landed upside down in the river's frigid waters.

Although the water was only about 4 feet (1.2 m) deep, the Honda Accord's doors jammed shut and several windows shattered. In the darkness, with icy water pouring into the car, Andersen was unable to locate the children quickly.

He quickly made the difficult decision to save himself, realizing that otherwise they might all perish.

Andersen freed himself from his seat belt, squeezed out a broken window, and swam to the surface. As he gasped for air, he saw motorists who had seen the accident rushing to his aid. One of them, Chris Willden, was a former police officer and military sniper. Trained to fire a gun underwater, Willden grabbed his pistol and carefully shot out a window, but was still unable to reach the children. At that point, enough people had gathered that they were able to use the water's buoyancy to turn the car right-side-up. One of the girls had found a pocket of air, but the other two, a 9-year-old girl and a 4-year-old boy, were facedown in the water, and the boy was not breathing. Willden used his pocketknife to cut the seat belts, and another passerby started CPR.

After a brief hospital stay, the kids were released and went on to celebrate the luckiest New Year ever.

SURVIVE A PLUNGE INTO WATER One of the scariest and most dangerous vehicle scenarios involves being trapped in a submerged vehicle. Whether your truck slid off an icy road into a frozen lake or your car went off the bridge into a river, the risk of being trapped in the vehicle and drowning is high when looking at water landings.

In situations like these, it's easy to panic, wasting precious time and air. One way to stay calm is to focus on specific, critical tasks. After the initial impact with the water, your first priority is to get your seat belt off. Instruct any passengers to do the same. Roll down one window, get a big lungful of air from the car's not-yet-flooded cabin, and climb out. Swim to the surface, and make sure everyone is out. Be prepared to swim to shore, potentially pulling others with you if you're able. If you leave the car's lights on, it will be easier for potential rescuers to find the vehicle, which is helpful even if everyone has made it to safety.

T / F

POWER WINDOWS WILL WORK UNDER WATER

TRUE While it might seem logical that water would short out your windows, in fact many electrically powered systems and components in the modern automobile can continue operating in the event of a submerged vehicle accident. If the battery is still operational as the car goes under, the electrical system could continue to work for up to three minutes (not that you have three minutes to spare!). Try the window button as soon as the vehicle has hit the drink and you are out of your seat belt. If it doesn't work, be prepared to break the window with your escape tool. Try to get out before the car goes under.

SKILL

YOUR CAR CAN BE A ROLLING SURVIVAL KIT. KEEP YOUR TRUNK FILLED WITH VITAL SUPPLIES LIKE FOOD, WATER, TOOLS, BLANKETS, AND OTHER CRUCIAL GEAR; AND YOU'LL BE READY FOR MOST EMERGENCIES.

STEER OUT OF A SKID A car starts to skid or spin out when it loses traction between the tires and the surface of the road. Often caused by slippery roads or bald tires, skids can be corrected—even once they've already started—and accidents can be avoided. Here's how to handle your vehicle—and yourself—if you feel the wheels losing their grip on the road.

STEP ONE Stay calm (this may be easier said than done, but do your best) and take your foot off the gas.

STEP TWO Turn the wheel gently in the direction you want the front of the car to go.

STEP THREE If your vehicle has anti-lock brakes (ABS), press the brakes—firmly—while steering into the skid. If your vehicle does not have ABS, do not use the brakes.

STEP FOUR Continue to adjust until the vehicle is going straight again.

TEETERING ON THE EDGE Whether your automobile is dangling on the cusp of a cliff or wavering on the rail of a ravine, the wrong move will send you and your vehicle right over the edge. Though this scenario may be more common in heist and action movies than in real life, it does occasionally happen, so there are benefits to being prepared for even the most outlandish of possibilities. Slow and thoughtful movements are the key to escaping this terrifying predicament.

Carefully begin shifting the vehicle's weight (items, passengers, anything not nailed down) toward the end of the vehicle that is resting over land. This is a balancing act in which the right moves can tip the scale in your favor and the wrong move—well, as for the wrong move, let's just say that it's not the fall that kills you, it's the sudden stop.

YOUR EMERGENCY CAR KIT Stocking your vehicle with tools and supplies will provide you with great advantages in an unexpected roadside emergency. Turn your motor vehicle into a rolling survival warehouse by carrying these.

JUMPER CABLES A heavy gauge set of jumper cables and a second vehicle can get your car running in the event that your battery has lost its charge or it needs a little boost in cold weather.

TOW STRAP A nylon tow strap can get your car or truck out of a ditch, snow bank, or swamp if there is another vehicle to pull you out. Select a heavy strap with *no metal parts*. A tow chain or a strap with metal hooks on the end can kill someone if it breaks while under tension.

ROAD FLARES Let the other drivers know you are there by signaling with road flares. Some will burn for up to 30 minutes. These also make a great fire starter for severe weather conditions.

TIRE REPAIR KIT A tire plug kit consists of glue, a few tools, and some rubber/fiber strips which can be glued in place if there is a hole in your tire's tread. Use one rubber strip for little holes, use the whole bundle if there is a gaping hole. A can of tire mending spray is able to seal small holes in a flat tire, and reinflate the tire enough to get you to a repair shop.

TOOLS Whether repairs are simple or more complex, they will all require tools. Consider a socket set, hammer, wrenches, pliers, and automotive-grade duct tape for your car tool kit. Use these items to fix your ailing vehicle or for other survival tasks.

WATER For your drinking water and for radiator fill ups, keep several gallons of water in your ride. Keep more than that if you live in, or travel through, dry climates.

FIRST AID Sometimes the vehicle needs a repair, and sometimes a person needs to be patched up, too. A good first aid kit will serve you well, especially during an emergency.

FULL-SIZED SPARE, TIRE IRON, AND JACK Don't settle for a dinky little emergency tire. Get a full-sized spare tire for your vehicle, and include it when rotating your tires for better wear. Make sure to have a tire iron and jack to complete the job.

BLANKETS OR SLEEPING BAGS Ideally, you should have one of these items for each seat in your vehicle. This will cover every passenger and the driver, in the event of a cold weather car breakdown.

FLASHLIGHT WITH SPARE BATTERIES It gets dark underneath your vehicle, and even darker at night. Give yourself every advantage you can by keeping a flashlight or two, and some extra batteries, in the vehicle at all times. Rotate the batteries every season, so you know you'll always have them in case of trouble.

INTO THE WILD

THE CANYONS CLOSE IN TIGHTER AS THE SUN SLIPS BELOW THE HORIZON. IN THE GLOOM, ALL SENSE OF DIRECTION VANISHES AND IT DAWNS ON YOU. YOU ARE HOPELESSLY LOST. PANIC RISES. YOUR PULSE POUNDS. THEN THE FIRST RAINDROPS START TO FALL. CAN YOU SURVIVE THE LONG COLD NIGHT?

The wilderness is a place of raw beauty and a refuge for many of us as we struggle to find a place of tranquility in our fast paced, technology-dependent world. The wilderness is also the place where the natural world still exists—our native habitat, if you will. When we visit these wild places, we might even imagine what it would be like to live there, as our ancestors once did, never again setting foot on concrete or steel. But when you leave the safety net of modern life, you open yourself up to the very real hazards and threats that our ancestors faced.

While getting lost in the wild, or succumbing to starvation, injury, or animal attacks may sound like perils or adventure tales from long ago, these emergencies are very real, and they still happen in modern times. And if your problems are compounded—say getting lost and then getting hurt, or running out of food and then losing your gear—then the odds of surviving are not good. Most survivors can deal with one problem, but when problems pile up, you're in big trouble.

TELL SOMEONE Some of the worst historic and contemporary survival stories could have ended up being mere inconveniences, had the survivors told someone where they were going and when they were planning to return. Tell a responsible friend or family member all the details of your wilderness trip. Better yet, write it all down for them. Tell them exactly where you're planning to go, where you'll park your vehicle, what route you'll take in the wilderness, and when you expect to return. This way, if you don't make it back on time, a local search and rescue team can be mobilized quickly. Fast deployment means they will have a much better chance of a happy rescue, not a grim faced, body-recovery mission.

THE STATS

3,600 Number of lost persons incidents reported on wilderness hikes yearly.

$5 MILLION Yearly cost of search-and-rescue operations by the United States National Park Service.

3 DAYS Amount of time a human body can last without water before succumbing to dehydration.

100 MILES (161 KM) Maximum distance from which a signal mirror can be spotted in optimal conditions.

71 DAYS Duration of time Ricky McGee of Australia spent stranded in the Outback in 2006 after his car broke down.

10% Percentage of lost hikers who go missing for more than 24 hours.

58% Percentage of lost hikers who were hiking alone at the time.

100% Percentage of people who, without visual cues to aid them (such as the sun), will walk in circles.

SURVIVAL PRIORITIES In any critical situation, the first thing you should do is check in on a basic list of "survival priorities." These are the issues you need to tackle, organized by importance in a checklist that starts with the most pressing issues and spans to the lesser concerns. These survival priorities are a game plan for your success, helping you to tackle the worst problem first, then the next most serious item, and so on. Don't ignore the list in an emergency, or mix up the items on a whim. The list starts with shelter, because a lack of shelter could kill you within hours in a dire situation. Once your shelter is secured, then water becomes the next priority, as any human can last only last a few days without it. Following these come fire, food, and signaling. Yes, there are odd situations where the priorities must be re-sequenced, but items are never dropped from this life-saving list.

SHELTER Finding, creating, or using an existing shelter is the first physical priority in almost any survival situation.

Your clothing is your first line of shelter from the elements. In cold weather, each extra layer is like another insurance policy to keep you safe. And in sunny, hot situations, the clothing protects your skin from burning and it limits dehydration. If your clothing isn't adequate for the cold weather, add additional insulation. Stuff grasses, leaves or other fluffy material into your clothes to increase their shelter value.

When it's time to go to sleep, if you're lacking a sleeping bag or space blanket (you shouldn't be, but accidents do happen) you can construct a shelter from natural materials. You don't need tools or a building permit in a wilderness survival scenario, you just need some daylight to see, and some sticks and vegetation. Take ideas from the animal nests you've seen in nature, and create a small "people nest," one that you can just barely squeeze into. Make it open and breezy to combat the heat, or make it thick and fluffy to fight the cold. And when fighting the cold, never underestimate the power of a warm rock or hot water bottle in your bedding. Heat up a stone near the campfire so that it is toasty hot, but no danger to your skin or bedding. Hold

SKILL

A basic shelter can be made with two (or more if you can find them!) forked support sticks and one long pole.

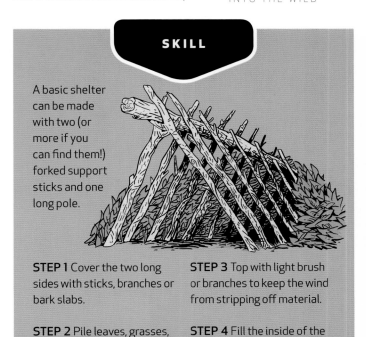

STEP 1 Cover the two long sides with sticks, branches or bark slabs.

STEP 2 Pile leaves, grasses, pine needles or debris over the frame.

STEP 3 Top with light brush or branches to keep the wind from stripping off material.

STEP 4 Fill the inside of the shelter with more vegetation, and crawl down inside.

it close and enjoy the radiating heat. Or pour hot water into a leak-proof bottle, stick it in a sock, and cuddle up with this time-tested bed warmer. These are two of the best wilderness tips in this book. You're welcome.

WATER Having safe and adequate drinking water is your second priority. Finding creeks and streams is easy enough in many parts of the world, but be aware that this water should be disinfected somehow. Catching rainwater, melting new snow, and locating a natural spring are a few ways to get safe drinking water without filters, fire, or chemical disinfectants. If there is any doubt about the water's safety, an easy method to treat the water is to boil it for 10 minutes. If you're lacking pots and pans to place over the flames, look for bottles or cans to use as boiling vessels. Fill them with water and place them in the ashes beside the fire; the water will soon start to boil. What you don't want to

WEAR SYNTHETIC FIBER OR WOOL FOR WARMTH AND DURABILITY, AND DON'T FORGET THAT YOU CAN STUFF YOUR CLOTHING WITH VEGETATION IF YOU NEED MORE INSULATION TO STAY WARM.

OUTDOOR GO BAG In the event you really need it, opening a well-stocked wilderness emergency kit should make you feel like it's Christmas morning. Everything you've been dying to have (literally) is right there within your grasp. Here's a minimum of what you should carry in your survival kit.

FIRESTARTERS Lighters, waterproof matches, and other fire makers should be scattered throughout your equipment.

HEATABLE CONTAINER A metal cup, bowl, or pot to boil in provides you a safe and unlimited water supply.

LIGHT Bring a light source like a flashlight or head lamp that is both rugged and waterproof.

SOUND Carry a whistle to signal for your buddies or to signal for help.

MIRROR Bring a signal mirror, which carries much further than the whistle.

WARMTH Stock an emergency shelter item like a space blanket or an emergency bivy sack.

KNIFE Carry a quality knife, for dozens of obvious reasons.

COMPASS Your GPS may not work, and you need to navigate.

FIRST AID You'll want to be ready to treat wounds and prevent infection

EMERGENCY FOOD Every extra bit of energy helps you survive. Fishing gear is a good backup strategy for when the food runs out.

WATER SAFETY Water purification tablets and a container for water should be on your list, as it's much easier to treat water with tablets than it is to boil it.

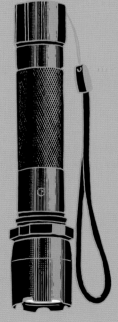

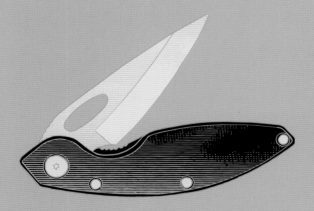

CAN'T DO WITHOUT

THE BUTANE LIGHTER If I only had one survival tool, depending on the scenario, I'd probably want it to be a lighter. The cheap and ubiquitous butane lighter is a ready source of flame, and you only need one working thumb to operate it. No matter how banged up your body has become, if your thumb's working, you can create a fire from a wide range of materials. One lighter has the potential to light hundreds, even thousands of fires. And a lighter can ignite materials that methods like spark rods and magnifying lenses could never hope to successfully kindle.

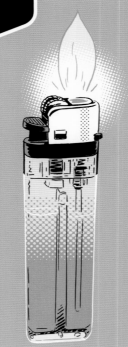

do is drink out of a ditch like some of the TV survival gurus often do on reality shows. Drinking water straight out of puddles, swamps, and the like is the fast track to dysentery, which can kill a healthy person in as little as a few weeks—painfully and embarrassingly.

FIRE Plain and simple, you should be carrying multiple fire-starting methods on your person on every outdoor excursion. Without this precious gear, improvising fire-starting equipment and lighting a fire would be a monumental task, or an impossible task under the worst of conditions. Fire can equal life in a variety of situations, and considering its myriad uses, from boiling water to heating, lighting, and cooking, it makes sense to carry several dependable fire starters. Keep a lighter in your pocket, matches in your backpack, and hang a spark rod on your key chain. It never hurts to learn some other techniques, too, like

T / F

YOU CAN'T EAT EVERYTHING ANIMALS DO

TRUE It turns out that despite our shared biology, there's a massive different between the human gastrointestinal tract and those of most animals. Some animals may be observed eating plants that are edible to humans, but these same animals can also eat plants that would be dangerous to a human. Birds are the worst animals to emulate, as they eat berries that can nourish us along with ones that could kill us. Even mammals like squirrels, who normally eat nuts that are safe as people food, will occasionally munch down on harmful mushrooms and nuts that are toxic to humans.

GO MODULAR! TURN EVERY KIT INTO A SURVIVAL KIT. ADD A LIGHTER AND SPACE BLANKET TO YOUR FIRST AID KIT. ADD WATER DISINFECTION GEAR AND A KNIFE TO YOUR VEHICLE REPAIR KIT. NOW THERE'S ALWAYS A SURVIVAL KIT ON HAND!

making a fire by concentrating sunlight through your glasses, or using primitive friction fire techniques. The point here is to have some primary methods at your disposal and have several backups in place, so you'll never be caught without your best friend in the wild.

FOOD Finding food is a lower priority than shelter, water, and fire, but it's the nagging, gnawing priority that becomes your full-time day job in mid-to-long-term survival situations. And trust me, it's not a fun job when you are scavenging just to stay alive in a bleak environment. If you don't know how to definitively identify the local wild edible plants, stick with animal foods. If it's got feathers, fur, scales, or a shell, there's a good chance it's safe to make into a meal. The feather and fur crowd is the safest bet. When killed and thoroughly cooked, even small birds and mini mammals provide a decent amount of calories and most are surprisingly tasty. Freshwater fish are another great food source, so much so that most survival kits come with a little fishing gear as standard equipment. Worms, crickets, termites, and many other critters are safe for human consumption, too. Just make sure that you cook them all thoroughly in case they are laden with parasites or disease-causing pathogens. Skip the nuts and berries, unless you're 100 percent certain of their identity and edibility. You don't want to play a round of poison wild berry roulette.

SIGNALING You have my permission to be obnoxious. Be loud, make a mess, and light stuff on fire. While this behavior may be frowned upon in the civilized world, it's exactly what you should do when signaling for help in the wilderness. You should have a cell phone, satellite phone, or personal locator beacon when you go into the deep wild, but if you don't, or if you lose signal or juice, here are three proven alternatives.

Probably the easiest and most well-known way to signal for help is with fire. Assemble the parts of your signal fire ahead of time in a large clearing or on a prominent high point, wait until someone is within sight, then light it up. The light and color of the flames can be a great signal at night, while thick smoke will work best during daytime. To get white smoke, light a hot blaze, then cover it up with plenty of live greenery. For gray or black smoke, throw on any plastics or oils that you may have access to.

Next, flares are a great addition to a survival kit. Handheld road-type flares are an option, but better is a small signal flare that will fire several hundred feet into the air. Larger flares or flare guns can achieve even greater heights and visibility. There is a downside to flares, however. You'll need to be extremely cautious when using them in dry conditions. That field of dry grass you're lost in? Not such a great place for flares. And rotate your flares annually, they don't last forever.

The flash of light from a mirror can also be a long-reaching option for a signal. If you have a mirror designed specifically for signaling, follow the directions that came with it. For other mirrors or reflective material, hold the mirror below your eye and at an angle that bounces light onto your outstretched fingers. Bring your illuminated digits slowly in line with the signaling target. Try tilting or rotating the mirror slightly, which will flash light to the signal target.

T / F

MOSS ALWAYS GROWS ON THE NORTH SIDE OF TREES

FALSE In my neck of the woods, I actually find more of the moss growing on the south side of the trees. This would lead me in a completely wrong direction if I confused my north and south navigation points. It turns out that my local moss species favor the southerly side of the trees because it's sunnier and warmer there, which is a good recipe for plant growth. But depending on the moss species and the local climate, the moss could be growing on any side of the tree—or on all sides. I'm sure this oft-quoted piece of folk wisdom works somewhere, but not everywhere.

COLD COMFORT

DAYS SHORTEN AND NIGHTS DARKEN. WATER AND FLESH FREEZE. WINTER IS COMING, AND WITH IT, THE SNOW AND ICE THAT CAN CRIPPLE OUR WORLD AND STEAL OUR LIVES. HOW DO YOU WIN THE FIGHT FOR WARMTH, IF THE POWER FAILS OR YOU ARE TRAPPED OUTSIDE? HERE'S HOW TO DO IT.

When we hear about someone dying from hypothermia (the lowering of the body's core temperature), we often imagine that it was some kind of extreme cold weather exposure that killed them. But in fact, the majority of hypothermia victims are found indoors, at temperatures slightly above freezing. There are several reasons for this unexpected and tragic statistic. Often, the victims are the elderly and the impoverished who cannot afford to buy heat in the winter. Drug and alcohol abuse also puts people in situations where it's easier to develop hypothermia.

The takeaway from these unfortunate losses is this one sobering idea: You don't have to be wandering in an arctic wasteland to die of hypothermia. This slow, cold demise can happen at temperatures above freezing, and it can happen in your very own apartment, house, or snowbound vehicle. If the heat goes out, the cold can kill within hours, and it does so without prejudice or preference, taking young and old, fit and fat, healthy and ill alike.

TEST FOR HYPOTHERMIA My cold weather rituals are numerous and diverse, which is likely the reason I still have my fingers and toes. But one ritual reigns supreme. A finger dexterity check can tell you as much (or more) than any other test. This assessment is quick, and can be performed at any time in cold conditions. Simply touch the tip of your thumb to the tip of each of your fingers (same hand). Assuming you can do this in warm weather, this full range of motion means that your forearms haven't locked up, and you are not hypothermic—not yet anyway. If you can't touch your pinky and ring finger, it means that muscles are locking up, and stronger hypothermia symptoms (like shivering, teeth chattering, and clumsiness) will soon follow.

95°F (35°C) Lowest temperature that the human body can reach before hypothermia begins.

56.7°F (13.7°C) Body temperature of Anna Bagenholm, who survived after being trapped under the ice of a frozen stream for 80 minutes in 1999.

95 FEET (29 M) Most snowfall recorded in one season, at Mt. Baker, Washington, U.S., from 1998–1999.

-133.6°F (-92°C) Coldest recorded temperature on Earth, at a ridge in east Antarctica.

15 INCHES (38 CM) Diameter of largest snowflake ever documented, in 1887 at Fort Keogh, Montana.

689 Number of hypothermia-related deaths each year in the United States.

4 INCHES (10 CM) Minimum ice thickness that can support a person.

RIDE OUT A BLIZZARD AT HOME Your own home should be the easiest place in which to weather a winter storm. With the comfort of familiar things around you, you just have to focus on staying warm, watered, and fed.

The planning and prep you have done before the storm should give you everything you need to shelter in place through a blizzard or ice storm. If the power goes out, and it probably will, your backups can handle all your needs. Use a wood stove or fireplace for heating, or a portable heater that's safe for indoor use. Keep several gallons (or liters) of water on hand per person in case your normal water supply freezes or fails. Don't forget to hang blankets and quilts over windows and doors for extra insulation.

Use your emergency lighting to read, write, play board games, or take care of survival chores. Battery-operated lights are safer than candles. You don't need to add a house fire to your existing blizzard emergency. Finally, try to be patient with yourself, your fellow "survivors," and the situation. The snow will all melt, eventually, whether you're calm or cranky. Calm is better.

WALK THROUGH A WHITEOUT It is very dangerous to walk through the blinding snow. There had better be a good reason for you to attempt it, because generally speaking, you want to stay put when you're in a blizzard. However, if an emergency calls for foot travel in a whiteout, here are some things you can do to stay safe. Put on appropriate outerwear, including parkas, mittens, face masks, and goggles. Make use of markers, like sticking a dark-colored pole into the snow every few yards (or meters) to create a visible path. Use a compass or GPS to stay on track. Or set up a long rope line to use as a "handrail" before the storm— say from your cabin to your outhouse.

DRIVE THROUGH A WHITEOUT Step one for driving through a whiteout is to rethink this crazy idea of driving through a whiteout. Step two is don't try to drive through a whiteout. But if there is some pressing need that cannot wait, then you may have to embark on a white-knuckled ride through the white stuff. Day or night, visibility and traction are the

GOOD TO KNOW

A CHILL IN THE AIR "Wind chill" describes the phenomenon wherein as the wind's speed increases, temperatures feel colder. This is a useful thing to keep in mind in extreme conditions, as wind chill can turn an uncomfortable temperature into a deadly one.

	5MPH 8KPH	10MPH 16KPH	20MPH 32KPH	30MPH 48KPH	40MPH 64KPH
32°F 0°C	26°F -3°C	22°F -6°C	18°F -8°C	16°F -9°C	14°F -10°C
20°F -7°C	13°F -11°C	9°F -13°C	4°F -16°C	1°F -17°C	-1°F -18°C
10°F -12°C	1°F -17°C	-4°F -20°C	-9°F -23°C	-12°F -24°C	-15°F -26°C
0°F -17°C	-11°F -24°C	-16°F -27°C	-22°F -30°C	-26°F -32°C	-29°F -34°C
-10°F -23°C	-22°F -30°C	-28°F -33°C	-35°F -37°C	-39°F -39°C	-43°F -42°C
-20°F -29°C	-34°F -37°C	-41°F -41°C	-48°F -44°C	-53°F -47°C	-57°F -49°C
-30°F -34°C	-46°F -43°C	-53°F -47°C	-61°F -52°C	-67°F -55°C	-71°F -57°C

FROSTBITE IN 30 MINUTES — FROSTBITE IN 10 MINUTES — FROSTBITE IN 5 MINUTES

IT MAY SEEM LOGICAL TO TIGHTEN YOUR BOOTLACES AS THE TEMPERATURE DROPS, BUT IF YOU DO THE OPPOSITE YOU'LL HAVE BETTER CIRCULATION AND WARMER FEET. THIS MAY EVEN SAVE YOUR TOES FROM FROSTBITE.

two biggest problems when driving in these conditions. You can help other crazy drivers to see you by keeping your hazard flashers on for the entire trip. But as far as your own ability to see, it will depend entirely on the conditions.

SKILL

TREAT FROSTBITE

Frostbite occurs when ice forms in your skin and tissues. Skin will often go numb right before frostbite. Then later (when the tissues thaw out), there's intense burning pain, and possibly lasting tissue damage.

Superficial frostbite occurs in patches, which may look dull in color, waxy, and pale. In deep frostbite, the skin will be pale and firm and the underlying tissues will feel solid.

To treat it, rewarm the skin and tissues (unless there is a danger of re-freezing). For superficial frostbite, place a warm body part against the frostbitten tissue. Deep frostbite requires hot water at stable temperatures (around 105° F [41°C]). Treat with pain meds as you begin rewarming. Do not rub frostbitten areas.

Be sure to protect that tissue from refreezing.

Make sure you have a full reservoir of low-temperature washer fluid, to help keep your windshield clean. And if conditions worsen and you cannot see, pull over in a safe place and keep your flashers on to reduce the risk of collision. Make the best of the situation, and it doesn't hurt to be prepared to enter a snowbound vehicle scenario.

SURVIVE A SNOWBOUND CAR I told you not to drive in a whiteout. But maybe, to your credit, you simply crashed into a snowbank. Either way, you're stuck in your car, surrounded by snow. This situation takes a turn for the worse when the vehicle cannot be seen, or if it's stuck in an untraveled area. But cheer up, this is a survivable event.

The vehicle provides you with a form of shelter, albeit a cold one. And if you've stocked your car for winter emergencies, then you should have plenty of gear. The first step is to call for help. Most folks have a cell phone these days, and you should always have a car charger, too. If no help is coming, bundle up for warmth and try to dig the vehicle out (if possible). Make sure the vehicle is stocked with warm clothing and outerwear, as well as some kind of shovel (a snow shovel is ideal). If the dig-out fails or isn't possible in the first place, hunker down in your car. High-energy food, water, and sleeping bags should be standard equipment for cold weather travel. Add a small bucket with a tight-fitting lid and some hygiene products, in case you're stuck in the car so long that you need a bathroom. Run the engine for warmth, occasionally, if you can keep the exhaust pipe clear. Create some kind of signal outside the vehicle so that you can be spotted by passersby. And never wander off to look for help. People who stay with the car generally make it, and those who don't are often lost.

IF YOU'RE LOST IN THE WOODS This can be the worst situation out of the bunch, as that beautiful winter wonderland quickly becomes a brutal frozen deathtrap. Survival when you're lost in cold, inhospitable conditions requires the right skills, actions, and materials. First, tackle the task of shelter. Build a snow cave, snow trench, lean-to, igloo, or whatever your skills and the available tools and

ICE RESCUE TOOLS Store bought or homemade, an ice rescue set is the most important tool around ice-encrusted waters. The set allows you to drive in spikes as moveable handholds, which can pull a person out of a hole in the ice. To make your own, assemble a hacksaw, drill, two ice picks with wooden handles, and 6 feet (2 m) of cord. Cut off half of the metal of each pick, at an angle, so that it is still pointed when you're done cutting. Drill a hole in each handle, tie the rope to each pick, and carry this with you every trip onto the ice.

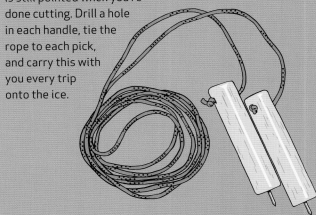

materials allow. Second, get a fire going. This may be very difficult in the snow, but it is possible. Create a "raft" or platform of green, freshly cut wood on top of the snow. Use thick or rotten pieces of broken wood if you have no cutting tool. Then build your fire on top of this structure, to keep your bed of coals away from the melting snow. Start the fire with dead evergreen twigs, gathered close to the trunks of snow-covered trees. These twigs will be drier, and they are full of resinous pitch, which will help them to burn better in the cold temperatures. Third, melt some snow for drinking water. Fill a non-plastic bottle, cup, or can with fresh snow and place it near the fire to melt. And finally, start signaling for help. Your fire is a good signal, but don't stop there. Use

A STIFF DRINK WILL KEEP YOU WARM

FALSE I hate to be the one to tell you, but that lovable Saint Bernard dog with a cask of rum around its neck isn't doing anyone any favors. Why not? Because even low-proof alcohol dehydrates the body (wasting water) and causes flushing of the skin (wasting heat). These effects make a person much more vulnerable to hypothermia. Alcohol can also cause difficulty walking, memory lapses, and impulsive behavior, all of which are dangerous in a survival situation. And when the booze wears off, a person is often left tired and confused. Couple the physiological effects of alcohol with a cold weather scenario, and you have a cocktail for disaster.

STAY DRY TO STAY WARM. SINCE MOISTURE CONDUCTS AWAY BODY HEAT, DO EVERYTHING YOU CAN TO KEEP YOUR CLOTHING AND OUTERWEAR DRY. STAY OUT OF THE WATER, AND TRY NOT TO BREAK A SWEAT IN COLD WEATHER.

any other methods at your disposal. Try using your cell phone until the battery dies. Blow a signal whistle, in an SOS pattern (3 short, 3 long, 3 short), until you can't stand it anymore. Use dark logs to spell HELP or SOS in the white snow. Do whatever you can to get noticed, because that's your ticket home.

IF YOU FALL THROUGH THE ICE Even thick ice can be pocked with thin spots, which occasionally give way and drop a skater or ice fisherman into the near-freezing water. Quick action and the right tools are your best bet for survival. If you're on the ice in the first place, you should have ice rescue spikes on your person—if you're skating on a pond or lake, someone should at least have a rope nearby. If you're rescuing yourself with the picks, get to the edge of the solid ice and stab both picks into the ice. Use all your strength to haul yourself out of the hole. Then use the spikes, hand over hand, to crawl away from the hole. Once you're several yards (or meters) from the hole, make for shelter and dry clothing as fast as you can. Be alert for the signs of both hypothermia and shock. In the event you are rescuing someone from the ice, tie off a rope to a secure object and carry (or throw) the rope out to the victim. There should be a loop tied in the end of the rope to help him hang on. Haul him out of the hole, get him into a warm place, and monitor for hypothermia and shock.

Three Days in the Snow

Underdressed and ill-prepared, a man from Nome, Alaska barely survived after getting his truck stuck in a snow drift and spending days below freezing temperatures. The 52-year-old took a drive on Monday, December 5th, 2011, without mentioning his plans to anyone. Far from town, his pickup slid into a deep snowdrift, becoming hopelessly stuck. The overnight low temperature was about -12°F (-24°C) that first night, not counting the wind chill.

Beyond cell-phone service, he realized that he was stuck until someone found him. Hours turned into days as he waited. Snow drifted, covering most of the truck. He occasionally ran the vehicle for heat, but by the third day, the gasoline was nearly gone. His only resources in the truck were a trash bag, a towel, a knife, and a few cans of frozen beer.

What saved him? Besides the slushy frozen beers slurped down for hydration, he had always been a very punctual employee. His manager and coworkers realized he was missing and contacted the local police on day two. After hours of searching on the third day, a search team spotted the bumper of the truck, and found the man alive—and 16 pounds (7 kg) lighter after shivering for 60 hours.

TWISTER

THE WIND ROARED WITH RAW FURY, THEN IT ALL WENT SILENT. CELLAR DOORS OPENED AND BEWILDERED PEOPLE EMERGED. A CAR SAT IN A TALL TREETOP, PERCHED LIKE A HUGE, GROTESQUE BIRD. ONE HOUSE STOOD UNTOUCHED, WHILE THE FIVE AROUND IT LAY IN RUIN. WELCOME TO TORNADO ALLEY.

Tornadoes occur on every continent except for remote Antarctica, but the United States is the nation where they strike the most. This is due to America's size, central flatlands, and intersecting weather patterns.

Though tornadoes happen in all 50 states, an area known as "Tornado Alley" typically experiences the most each year. This area covers much of Arkansas, Iowa, Kansas, Louisiana, Minnesota, Nebraska, North Dakota, Ohio, Oklahoma, South Dakota, and Texas. The high concentration of twisters is due to cold air dropping from Canada and colliding with the warm, tropical air of Mexico and the dry air from the Southwest.

This clash of weather systems sets a chain reaction in motion, one that often ends with twisters ripping their way through property and lives. Finding a safe shelter is the best refuge. This could be a specially constructed storm cellar, an ordinary basement, or even a ditch if you get caught outside.

SIGNS OF DANGER Tornadoes aren't always an obvious funnel shape dropping down from an dull-green angry sky. Sometimes the funnel isn't visible, if it's free of debris and moisture. If a tornado watch is in effect, or a tornado is suspected, look for the following signs. During daylight hours, you may see thick stormy clouds with a strong, constant rotation at the base. Another sign is whirling dust or debris on the ground under a storm cloud, caused by a tornado that isn't visible. At any time, listen for a loud continuous rumble that sounds like a train approaching and doesn't fade like thunder. At night, you may also see small, bright flashes at ground level near a thunderstorm (that don't look like streaks of lightning). This could be power lines snapping, broken by the high winds of a tornado.

THE MATRIX

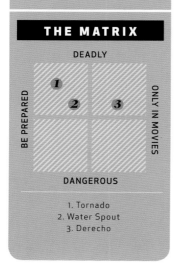

DEADLY

BE PREPARED

ONLY IN MOVIES

DANGEROUS

1. Tornado
2. Water Spout
3. Derecho

SHELTER IN PLACE, PROPERLY Where do you run, where do you hide? If you're already having a bad luck day and a twister is coming to get you, then you don't want to take any chances by choosing any old shelter spot. Pick the safest and sturdiest spot you can get to quickly. No matter where you shelter, use this basic body protecting technique: Crouch down low with your face downward. Cover your head with your hands, or throw on a sports helmet for protection against head injury if at all possible. Wrap up in blankets or sleeping bags to pad against bodily injury, or flop a mattress on top of you for storm debris protection. Here are some options for hunkering sites.

IN A HOUSE If you're in a house with a basement, by all means go down there and crawl under some kind of sturdy protection. This could be a heavy table, a work bench, a mattress, or the like. Stay keenly aware of the position of heavy objects (like refrigerators, waterbeds, pianos, etc.) on the floor above the basement, and don't hang out under those spots. Also, avoid windows and sliding glass doors.

If you're in a house with no basement, a dorm, or an apartment, the first rule is to stay away from the windows. Go to a bathroom, closet, or a space under the stairs on the lowest floor. Failing that, get to an interior hallway with no windows. Alternately, jumping into a bathtub may offer partial protection, but cover up with some sort of thick padding, like a mattress or several blankets, to cushion you from falling debris.

IF YOU'RE IN A MOBILE HOME Run for your life! No mobile home or trailer is as safe as a permanent, sturdy building (or a storm cellar). If you live in a trailer or similar dwelling, make tornado evacuation plans ahead of time by selecting a nearby permanent structure for your shelter site. Even small tornadoes can destroy tied-down mobile homes. Don't take any chances. Even the best built and most modern of mobile homes and trailers cannot handle the high winds and incredible wrenching forces of tornadoes. The two main weaknesses of these abodes are the open space under the trailer and the lightweight building materials. The space

GOOD TO KNOW

NAME THAT STORM
Tornadoes come in a surprising number of shapes and sizes besides the classic land-bound twister of movie and TV fame. Here are some other related phenomena to be aware of.

WATERSPOUT Just what it sounds like, this is the term for what happens when tornado conditions occur over water. Most common in the Florida Keys and the Adriatic Sea.

LANDSPOUT OR DUST DEVIL Term for a tornado that is not associated with a thunderstorm.

DERECHO As compared with the traditional "twister" shape of a tornado, the derecho is a powerful straight-line windstorm that accompanies major thunderstorms. They occur in warm weather around the world.

underneath can allow the wind under the trailer, which can end up flipping it or lifting it into the air. The lightweight construction that makes these dwellings moveable also enables the tornado to move them, occasionally shredding them into tiny pieces. Flee a mobile home if there is a threat of tornado in your area, and seek shelter in a sturdy building immediately. Even if the building is a store or some other business, hang out there until the danger has passed.

AWAY FROM HOME In a church, theater, mall, or large store, seek shelter as quickly as possible in an interior bathroom, storage room, or some similar small enclosed area away from any windows. I once got notice that there was a nearby tornado while I was shopping in a large home improvement store. The management made the right call by ushering all of the staff and customers to the back of the store and away from the large front windows. I hung out by the bathtubs, just in case things went bad. Thankfully, they didn't. If you're at school, follow the staff's instructions. This should be to go to an interior hall or room. Avoid windows and large open spaces like gyms and auditoriums.

T/F

A TORNADO CAN FLING A FORK HARD ENOUGH TO EMBED IT IN A TREE

TRUE It's common to see post-tornado photos of vinyl records stuck halfway into a telephone pole, or forks sunk deep into a tree. These aren't fake—at the same time that tornado winds are flinging debris off at hundreds of miles (or kilometers) per hour, those forces are also twisting trees and telephone poles, and soaking them in rain. The wet wood fibers separate, the debris sinks in, and when the winds stop the result is a very terrifying sculpture.

A STORM CELLAR A storm cellar can be a modified basement or a purpose-built haven where you can weather the worst. It should be very close to your home, if it's a separate structure. Make certain that it's always unlocked, and that the doors can be fastened down securely from the inside. You don't want to be fumbling for keys when a twister comes calling. Keep some drinking water and shelf-stable food down there too, in case the area is decimated when you emerge.

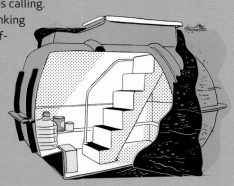

IF A CAR IS YOUR ONLY SHELTER This is a dicey one. Sheltering in vehicles is a risky gambit in a tornado. Vehicles can be tumbled or thrown by a strong twister. It really boils down to a choice of similar perils. If you see a tornado while you're driving in a car, and it's far away and you have open road in front of you, you may be able to outdistance the disturbance by driving at right angles to the tornado's path (if you can tell what that is). Of course, the smarter choice is to seek shelter in a durable building or in an underground spot, if possible.

If you're caught in a vehicle and cannot drive, the best option is usually to abandon that vehicle. Statistically speaking, you're safer when lying in a ditch than you are sitting in the car. If you do decide to stay in the car, or you don't have time to run to a ditch, keep your seat belt fastened, cover your head with your hands, and use a jacket, coat, or some other covering to protect you from flying debris. The vehicle will be safer on a lower road level than a higher one or on a bridge. That said, you should still avoid sheltering under bridges and overpasses. The wind is often amplified and turbulent in these areas, creating a deadly trap.

CAUGHT OUT IN THE OPEN Getting caught out in the open during a tornado may not be the death sentence that it would seem to be at first blush. If you get caught outdoors, and there is no sturdy shelter within running distance, lie flat and face-down in a low area. Protect the back of your head with your arms and any extra clothing you may have. Don't try to hold onto a trees, or shelter near other seemingly solid objects. They may be blown onto you, or you may be scooped up and hurled at them.

DEAL WITH A DOWNED POWER LINE A supreme hazard in the aftermath of a tornado or wind storm is downed power lines. Lethal amounts of electricity can still be flowing through the lines, ready to turn storm survivors into secondhand casualties. This one's easy: Stay far, far away from any utility lines on the ground. If you suspect that any utilities are damaged, notify the local authorities.

TORNADOES CAN HAPPEN ANY DAY (OR NIGHT) OF THE YEAR. IF YOU LIVE IN AN AREA OF THE U.S. WHERE TORNADOES ARE LIKELY, KEEP A NOAA WEATHER RADIO IN YOUR HOME, WITH LOUD ALERT TONES TO SIGNAL LOCAL EMERGENCIES.

HOUSE ON FIRE

COUGHING AND SWEATING, YOU TOSS AND TURN—SUDDENLY, A SHRILL ALARM AWAKES YOU. YOU SCOOP YOUR CHILDREN FROM THEIR UPSTAIRS BEDS, BUT THE STAIRWAY LEADING DOWN IS FILLED WITH FLAME. THE HOME YOU KNOW AND LOVE IS SUDDENLY TRYING TO KILL YOU.

Fire can be our friend, one of the vital elements in wilderness survival scenarios, but it can also be a terrible force, both damaging and deadly. Fire can devour our homes and businesses, turning our hard-earned material wealth into ashes.

Once flames have broken out, time becomes incredibly precious. A hidden smouldering blanket can suddenly burst into a terrifying nightmare of choking smoke and searing heat.

The worst part of this particular threat is its total unpredictability. A terrible fire may never happen to you—or, even if you try to do everything right, it may happen several times in your life. We had a chimney fire when I was a child. I don't remember much about it, just the damage afterward, but it made a huge change in my parents' attitude toward fireplaces and wood stoves. And these aren't the only sources of possible ignition. Cooking fires, electrical fires, clothes dryer fires, and many other types of fire can hit us out of nowhere and start a home-leveling blaze.

DON'T BE A HERO! Chances are good that some of you reading these words are (or have been) firefighters. I'd like to thank you for your bravery and service to others. The rest of us, however, haven't been through that training. We don't understand how dangerous the smoke and gasses of a house fire really are. We don't know how quickly and ferociously a home can be consumed by fire. We don't know fire's behaviors, how it climbs, spreads, and breathes. And not knowing all this, our only job in a fire is to grab the people in our homes and flee a house fire as fast as our legs can carry us. Once the humans are safely outside, use your cell to call 911. Let the professionals fight the fire and find your frightened pets.

THE STATS

56% Percentage of house fires resulting from cooking accidents.

5% Estimated percentage of U.S. homes that are equipped with fire extinguishers.

$7.5 BILLION Annual cost of fire and burn injuries.

374,000 Average number of yearly house fires in the United States.

7 Daily average number of fatalities resulting from house fires in the U.S.

1,100°F (593°C) Average temperature of a burning house fire.

THE MATRIX

DEADLY

BE PREPARED

ONLY IN MOVIES

DANGEROUS

1. House Fire
2. Grease Fire
3. Electrical Fire
4. Chemical Fire

House fires are menacing and life-changing events. As the fire takes hold of wood and cloth, it turns a normally safe sanctuary into a mindless killer. To prevent this scenario from claiming your household, exercise these strategies of fire prevention and fire escape.

FIRE PREVENTION Detecting possible fire hazards is the first step in creating a safer home. Periodically inspect your home for overloaded electrical outlets and power strips. Make sure that children don't have access to matches, lighters, and other fire starters. Keep flammable materials like kitchen towels and paper away from stoves. Clean the dryer vents seasonally, to prevent the buildup of flammable fibers. Replace gas appliances if they begin to show faults, particularly failing pilot lights. And to prevent burn injuries and help save the lives, smoke alarms are the best tool in the home. Make sure you have a functional smoke alarm in every area of the home. These affordable alarm devices should be mounted high on the wall or on the ceiling in the kitchen, the basement, and in every bedroom. Replace all of the batteries annually, and replace the units themselves every decade. Not convinced? More than 60 percent of house fire deaths happen in dwellings without working smoke alarms.

FIRE EXTINGUISHERS If prevention efforts fail, there may be a golden moment when you can stop a small fire. Fire extinguishers have saved countless lives and properties, but they aren't foolproof or magical. It pays to know how to properly operate a modern fire extinguisher and which type to have. When should you try to use an extinguisher? After you've made sure that others in the home are safe, and only if the fire is small with minimal smoke. Be ready to call 911 if the extinguisher doesn't do the trick.

YOUR FAMILY PLAN Your fire escape plan could be the most important plan that you and your family ever create, so design it carefully and pay attention to the details. First of all, pick an official meeting spot for your family, the place that you all know to head for if you get separated—a

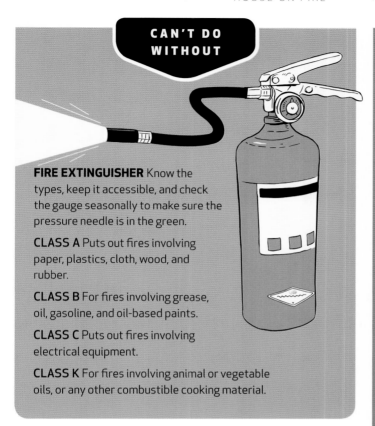

CAN'T DO WITHOUT

FIRE EXTINGUISHER Know the types, keep it accessible, and check the gauge seasonally to make sure the pressure needle is in the green.

CLASS A Puts out fires involving paper, plastics, cloth, wood, and rubber.

CLASS B For fires involving grease, oil, gasoline, and oil-based paints.

CLASS C Puts out fires involving electrical equipment.

CLASS K For fires involving animal or vegetable oils, or any other combustible cooking material.

NEVER THROW WATER OR FLOUR ON A GREASE FIRE (THERE WILL BE EXPLOSIVE RESULTS). USE AN EXTINGUISHER, THROW BAKING SODA ON IT, OR DROP A LARGE METAL LID ON THE FIERY PAN. FLEE AND CALL 911 IF THIS FAILS.

neighbor or relative's house, or a close-by police or fire station, church, or school. Next, designate the family member who, in an emergency, has been chosen to head for a neighbor's house to call for help. Even if your cell phones are working, there's no harm in having a firm plan for one specific call to be made from a landline.

As a group, figure out your escape plan. Ideally, the plan should involve multiple escape possibilities from every room of the house (in case the main doors or hallways are blocked by smoke or fire). In multistory homes, you might want to consider purchasing a simple escape ladder that can be dropped from a second-story window or balcony. As a family, do fire drills a couple of times a year, and practice low crawling to get out of the house, stop-drop-and-roll, and escaping in the dark.

MEAN STREETS

THE AGE-OLD GAME OF PREDATOR AND PREY CONTINUES, BUT THE HUNTING GROUNDS ARE ALL BRAND NEW. WITH BLADE AND GUN, OPPORTUNISTS COME TO HUNT, IN PACKS OR AS LONE PREDATORS, FOR OUR MONEY OR OUR BLOOD. THE CRIMINALS ARE HUNTERS, AND WE ARE THEIR PREY.

Violence is nothing new. On some level, I'd say that we as a species have a taste for it. Our ancestors fought over land, water, wealth, and ideas. And our contemporaries still do the same. Little has changed over the millennia. For every group of peaceful people, there is a wolf among the sheep. And even the peace-loving, when pushed too far, will snap and fight for what they need.

It's been said that man is the deadliest animal, and there's no shortage of backup for that idea. Check out the news for your local examples of people who turned into predators. So what do we do about it? And how do we fight back against those human animals who have gone bad? Through avoidance, awareness, distraction, evasion, and self-defense—in that order.

Don't mix this sequence up, and always see fighting as a last resort. Just because you took a martial arts class once or are pumped up from watching an action flick doesn't mean that you should jump right into a fight or take chances that can be avoided.

DROP A DROP WALLET If your money is all muggers and thieves are after, there's a clever way to give them some and still keep most of it for yourself. Drop wallets have been successfully used as decoys all over the crime-ridden world, and they're a great trick for getting back home with most of your dough. The next time you upgrade your wallet, keep the old one. Put two or three dollars in it, and the fake credit cards that came with your new wallet. Carry both with you when you head out into public. In the event of a mugging, throw the old wallet as a decoy and take off running in the other direction. The thief should go for the wallet, especially if they saw the money and cards as it flew by. Bonus points if you include a photo of your girlfriend in Canada.

THE STATS

8 P.M. TO 3 A.M. Period of time during which most muggings occur.

25% Relative higher likelihood of being mugged in London than in Harlem.

50 Number of children mugged daily in London— mostly for their mobile phones.

3 Number of mugging-related fatalities in New York City annually.

44.5% Percentage of robberies that are confrontational or violent.

90% Percentage of suspects arrested for robbery who are male.

5 Age of youngest mugger on record.

449,246 Number of robberies (including muggings and violent theft, excluding pickpocketing and extortion) recorded by police in the U.S. in 2006.

354,520 Number of robberies recorded by police in the U.S. in 2012.

BE AWARE OF YOUR SURROUNDINGS Situational awareness is the bread and butter of crime prevention. Simply put, it's a combined ability to pay attention to details, process the information you gain, use this information to identify threats, and create plans to handle the threats or avoid them. This is the same mental multitasking that military and law enforcement professionals use when on duty. They are paying attention to everything, especially the individuals and situations that look like trouble. While the training that brought these professionals to their alert status is not available to the public, we can all take steps to develop a more alert mental state. Enhance your own natural powers of observation with these three simple acts.

First, eliminate distractions. Chatting on your cell phone or listening to music through headphones may seem harmless enough, but they are poison to situational awareness. Reading in public and playing games on your phone are also likely to rob you of the attention you should be paying to your surroundings.

Next, look at people. Don't make eye contact with strangers (who may perceive your stare as a threat), but check out the people around you wherever you go. Pay attention to the body language and actions of the people around you.

Finally, look at your surroundings. Whether you are in the city or the wild, it makes sense to pay attention to the lay of the land. Understand where you are, where you are going, and which way to go if you need to backtrack. And while you're at it, assess any possible dangers.

CAUSE A DISTRACTION Assuming your situational awareness failed you, or an assailant comes at you from nowhere, it's time to try distraction. While a few crooks are bright, the rest are not. Drugs and alcohol can also take their toll on a criminal's cognitive ability. A friend of mine once hurled a hot burrito at a man who was harassing her, giving her the time to duck into a nearby store. Distractions may not always work, but successfully distracting the bad guy can give you the opportunity to dive right into our next tactic: evasion.

SKILL

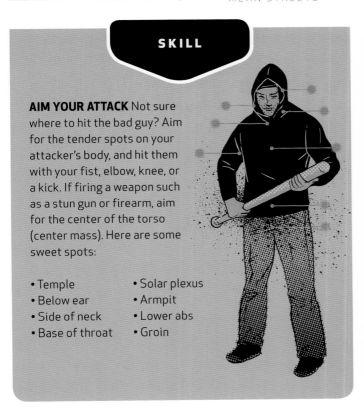

AIM YOUR ATTACK Not sure where to hit the bad guy? Aim for the tender spots on your attacker's body, and hit them with your fist, elbow, knee, or a kick. If firing a weapon such as a stun gun or firearm, aim for the center of the torso (center mass). Here are some sweet spots:

- Temple
- Below ear
- Side of neck
- Base of throat
- Solar plexus
- Armpit
- Lower abs
- Groin

BRAVELY RUN AWAY Bolt away, slink away, climb away, just get some distance between you and the bad guy. Call 911. Then, hide somewhere with people, if you can. Places like a store, a café, or someplace with police or guards are your best bets. Don't try to hide in a dark alleyway or a secluded restroom, things will only get worse if the pursuer finds you in there. If you can blend into a press of people, do so—and try to radically alter your appearance as you enter the mix. Drop your coat or jacket, especially if you're wearing a different color underneath. Change your hair, ditch your hat, put on sunglasses, do whatever you can to look like a completely different person. Change direction often, and call 911 for help when you get a chance. And when you're going out on the town, wear shoes that allow you to run in the event of an attack, and outerwear loose enough to wriggle out of if someone tries to grab you.

A QUICK YELL CAN OFTEN BRING YOU SOME ASSISTANCE. IF YOU YELL "HELP," "THIEF," "RAPE," OR "FIRE," AS IS APPROPRIATE IN A PUBLIC PLACE, YOU MAY GARNER ASSISTANCE AND DISTRACT YOUR ASSAILANT.

FIRE WARNING SHOTS TO SCARE BAD GUYS AWAY

FALSE Unless you're roaming a bleak, futuristic wasteland, the laws governing self-defense are still in effect. Using a firearm to scare someone is called brandishing—it's illegal, and it makes you look like the bad guy in court. Shooting only to wound, or firing warning shots, can lead to more legal trouble. Using a firearm in a non-lethal way may seem like the right choice in a scary situation. But in truth, you've fired prior to being under actual threat. Don't draw any weapon unless you honestly believe you are in immediate danger. Then, do what you've trained to do: shoot your attacker's center mass.

UNARMED SELF-DEFENSE You tried distraction, you tried flight, the only thing left now is to fight. While we could devote a whole book series to the diverse arts of self-defense and street fighting, there's still something to be said for the survival instincts of an unarmed, unskilled, cornered animal (you!).

If you find yourself weaponless (bad idea), tap into that primal rage, and fight your attacker off like a wolverine fights off a bear. Even though the bear can weigh 10 times more than the wolverine, the snarling, snapping, biting, and scratching wolverine usually wins these fights through sheer savagery.

I'm not saying don't study martial arts; in fact, I'll recommend that you get some training. Find a dojo or boxing club near your home or work, and put in some hours, as many as you can. Learn to take a hit, and how to give them, effectively. And whether you follow through with training or not, never forget that feisty wolverine. When it comes to a fight, it's time to punch, elbow, kick, knee, gouge, scratch, rip, bite, scream, and snarl your way to a dirty street fight victory.

ARMED DEFENSE Don't be the guy bringing a knife to a gunfight, be the guy with the gun at the fistfight. If you're unlucky enough to get caught in an altercation or criminal act, you're ideally carrying a weapon. If your city or state allows concealed carry firearms, go through the training to carry a concealed weapon. Practice with that weapon often (weekly works well for many people). And don't get caught without it. Pepper spray and stun guns can also be helpful. Keep a good-sized knife handy, if you can't carry or do not wish to use the aforementioned weapons.

Whatever you may end up with, it's best to find a self-defense class that can train you to use the items you are likely to have on you. And failing all that, use whatever weapon you can lay your hands on. A roll of quarters is not too heavy and should be legal to carry anywhere, and it increases the power in a punch. A tactical pen or a regular pen can deliver a painful stab. Even a rolled-up magazine can strike and help to block a knife attack.

Wrong Place, Wrong Time

I was in the wrong place at the wrong time. Spoiler alert—I made it, but it could have gone very differently. I was driving home late, running on fumes, and had to pee. I stopped for gas, and asked the attendant about a bathroom. He pointed behind the building. After skirting the entire structure and finding no restroom, I realized that he meant for me to simply go behind the building. No sooner had I finished than a man in dark clothing jumped out of the bushes, yelling "Get on the ground! Get on the ground, now!" I was still fumbling with my zipper when he pushed me down on all fours, then a cold piece of metal was pushed hard against the base of my skull. When I both heard and felt the click, I realized that it was a gun. I didn't fight back. I didn't know how at the time. And it's actually a good thing I didn't (and a good thing my bladder was already empty). The man with the gun was a police officer in a dark uniform, who had been chasing two men who robbed the hotel next door. I fit the description of one of the men. After some detaining and explaining, I was free to go. And guess who pees before they leave, and gases up the car in daylight ever since then?

THE UNPREDICTABLE

*I*t's not every day that you get caught in an avalanche or become the victim of a home invasion, but in these terrifying and life threatening events, it's crucial to know what to do. This section will help you navigate some of the weirder situations the modern world may present to you. Some have warning signs that you can learn to identify, giving you precious time to escape—but a few situations can come at you from nowhere, forcing you to make quick decisions. You probably didn't see these troubles on the horizon when your day began, but that doesn't make you a helpless victim. With the right skills and techniques, you can become a serious contender in the fight for your life. And if you follow in the footsteps of the survivors before you, you just might make it out alive and in one piece.

TSUNAMI

A WALL OF CHURNING WATER RISES QUICKLY FROM THE LOW AND PLACID OCEAN. UNSTOPPABLE, IT RAMS HOTELS AND SHOOTS THROUGH THE OPEN STREETS. WE CANNOT OUTRUN THE HUNGRY MAW OF THIS MARITIME BEAST, BUT WE MAY CLIMB HIGHER THAN ITS LETHAL REACH.

Tsunamis are one of the weirdest and most frightening phenomena in nature. Few things can become phobia fodder like the idea of being swept away by a wall of water summoned from the deep.

The word tsunami is Japanese in origin, meaning "harbor wave," and tsunamis are also known as seismic sea waves. These waves occur when a large volume of water is displaced in the ocean—or in a large lake. Most commonly caused by earthquakes, tsunamis can also stem from volcanic activity, landslides, an impact from a space object (such as an asteroid), and the detonation of a nuclear weapon under the water. These disasters don't happen very often, but when they do, they are terrifying—and the results can be horrific.

Tsunamis cause damage in two ways. The first round of destruction comes from the impact of a wall of water traveling at high speed. Once the wave has crashed onto shore, the second form of damage occurs as the powerful volume of water moves across the land, laden with dangerous debris.

TAKE THE HIGH GROUND When you hear a tsunami warning, how high should you climb for safety? Is your second-floor hotel room high enough? What about the roof of the building next door? Should you instead retreat inland in search of higher elevation?

Since some of the biggest tsunamis can reach heights of 100 feet (30 m) above sea level, you'll want to get as high as you possibly can. At the beginning of every beach vacation or seaside retreat, take a moment of your time to consider escape routes and high locations within your reach. Make sure to find out if there are designated tsunami evacuation routes in the area. Always have a plan (or two) to reach higher ground, and stay alert to the warning signs of a tsunami.

THE STATS

230,000 Number of casualties from the 2004 Indian Ocean tsunami.

14 Highest number of countries affected by the same tsunami.

$235 BILLION Damages cost of the tsunami caused by the 2011 earthquake in Tohoku, Japan.

6 MILES (10 KM) Farthest distance that waves from the Tohoku earthquake tsunami reached inland.

80% Percentage of tsunamis that occur within the Pacific "Ring of Fire."

500 MPH (800 KPH) Top speed of a tsunami.

1,720 FEET (524 M) Tallest tsunami wave ever recorded, from the 1958 megatsunami in Ltuya Bay, Alaska.

8,000 MILES (12,800 KM) Longest distance traveled by tsunami waves propagated by the 2004 Indian Ocean quake, reaching to British Columbia, Canada.

Anytime you're in a coastal area, it's a good idea to think about where you would go in a big-wave emergency. The fear of tsunamis shouldn't stop you from enjoying a well-earned beach vacation; just realize that even a small tsunami can endanger a community by the water's edge.

SPOT TSUNAMI SIGNS The most important thing you can do is to be aware, and even a little jumpy. If you hear a tsunami warning, or notice any of the signs we're about to discuss, indicating that a tsunami may be coming, make your way to high ground. Worst case scenario, you look foolish but are still alive. Best case scenario, you are saved from an actual tsunami. The most obvious harbinger of a tsunami is an earthquake in a coastal region. Another thing to look out for is any change in animal behavior. Scientists believe critters pick up on the earth's vibrations before we do, so if they're nervous, it may be for good reason. Finally, receding water is the first sign of a tsunami reaching the land. If the waterline suddenly recedes dramatically, exposing normally submerged areas, you have less than five minutes before the "harbor wave" hits.

SURVIVE BEING SWEPT AWAY Getting caught up in a tsunami has been likened to being trapped in a raging river full of branches and sharp rocks. You're caught in a wild maelstrom along with a floating junkyard full of jagged metal, nail-studded lumber, raw sewage, twisted vehicles, panic-stricken animals, and dead bodies. How are you going to survive that?

First things first: avoid the face of the tsunami. The greatest force of a wave is in its breaking face. This roiling mass also carries the majority of pulverizing debris. If this catches you, try to hold on to something secure until this deadly part of the wave passes. Then, after the breaking face, you'll be hit with several waves. And with them come the double-edged sword of tsunamis: debris. These pieces may be deadly, or they may give you a fighting chance. Climb on top of anything that floats, and use it to reach a higher point. Once the water begins to drain, you're either going inland with the initial surge or being dragged out

If you need to add weight at one end of a rope, use this knot. When throwing it, stack the rope at your feet, starting with the end of the line you'll be holding, so it uncoils tangle-free.

STEP 1 Make two bights in the end—this results in three "rungs" of rope next to one another.

STEP 2 Weave the working end (leave plenty) under the middle rung and over the bottom rung, then loop it around the back to bring it between the top and middle rungs.

STEP 3 Wrap all three rungs 6–9 times. On the last wrap, thread the working end through the remaining loop and pull to tighten.

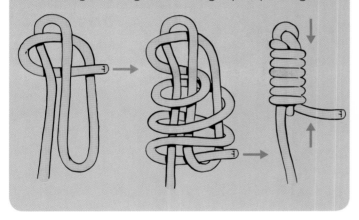

to sea. If it's the latter, keep the shore in sight and swim parallel to it as you would do to escape a rip current.

DEAL WITH A TSUNAMI AT SEA An odd but true survival fact is that one of the safest places you can be during a local tsunami is on a boat in deep water. If you get word of a quake while boating, immediately head for deeper water. When you're out in the ocean, the tsunami will be little more than a swell in most cases. If rough water does catch you, steer the boat up the wave and apply maximum throttle to climb the swell.

TSUNAMIS RARELY GIVE MUCH IN THE WAY OF WARNING. AN ODD TREMBLE OR TIDE MAY BE THE ONLY HINTS YOU GET. DON'T WASTE TIME IF YOU SUSPECT ONE IS ON THE WAY. SCOOP UP YOUR KIDS AND MAKE FOR HIGHER GROUND. RUN, DON'T WALK.

AVALANCHE ALERT

CRASHING SNOW, MUD, AND STONES SLIDE FROM THEIR PERCHES TO BURY THE UNSUSPECTING BELOW. QUICKLY AND WITHOUT REMORSE, THE EARTH WE STAND UPON CAN ENTOMB US. WHAT DO YOU DO WHEN YOUR FOOTING GIVES WAY AND NATURE TRIES TO SWALLOW YOU WHOLE?

Snow, mud, and rocks, though radically different in many ways, have one treacherous thing in common: They can bury you, not to mention kill you, with the same action and in a matter of moments.

Rock slides, avalanches, and mudslides are usually small, localized events, but they are fully capable of interring you six feet under (or deeper). While your response to each of these events may be a little different, there are some common ties between them.

First, remain vigilant and aware in areas where these hazards are a possibility. Second, avoid areas that look like they could be promising candidates for any kind of slide. And third, if you absolutely must cross an area that may give way, keep an eye out for sheltered spots where you would be able to take refuge in the event of a sudden catastrophe, such as huge trees and giant boulders you could hide behind. Sure, it's fun to scramble up a patch of scree or trek across a field of snow, but these outdoor adventures are not without their particular, deadly hazards.

KNOW YOUR SNOW How do you deduce that you're in an area prone to avalanches? There are many signs that can help you avoid becoming a human popsicle. Two of the biggest things to keep an eye on are recent heavy snowfall and the mountain's incline. Avalanche risks greatly increase after a heavy snowfall and changes in weather. The worst time of all is when snowy weather is followed by warm weather or rain—and then cold, snowy conditions return. The angle of the mountain slope is also a major player in this deadly game. Most avalanches occur when the slope is 30–45 degrees, but even slopes of 25 or 60 degrees can start to slide if the conditions are right (or, from your perspective, very, very wrong).

THE STATS

90% Percentage of snow avalanches triggered by the victim.

105 Yearly number of casualties of winter avalanches worldwide.

20,000 Record number of landslide victims, in 1970 at Mt. Huascaran, Peru.

4.79 CUBIC MILES (20 KM³) Greatest volume of earth displaced by a landslide, in Saidmarreh, Iran, around 10,000 B.C.E.

250 MPH (400 KPH) Fastest avalanche ever recorded, in the Mount St. Helens eruption in 1980.

THE MATRIX

1. Avalanche
2. Rockslide
3. Mudslide

Slides formed from snow, mud, and rock can be lethal and hard to predict. Keep your eyes peeled for the following signs and pay heed to these methods for getting out of harm's way.

SCOPE OUT AVALANCHE ZONES The aforementioned recent snowfall and slope angle are the most likely risk factors for avalanche, but there are a handful of other indicators. For one, there's the sun's position. Snow is most volatile on slopes that have melted and refrozen repeatedly. During warmer winter days, plan a route that keeps you off these slopes. Also, trust your ears and eyes. Don't tread on snow that makes a hollow sound when you step on it, or that looks like large, sparkly crystals instead of powder (this is deadly stuff called depth hoar). Keep a lookout for evidence, too—snow debris and broken trees are signs of previous avalanches, so be especially wary of these trouble spots. Also watch for "chutes without ladders," open, chute-like areas with no trees or rocks on the slope. That's because trees and boulders act as anchors for snowpack; when they're absent, it's more dangerous.

If you're hiking, stick to ridgelines, windward hillsides, dense forests, or low-angle slopes. If you're skiing, stay on groomed trails.

SWIM THROUGH AN AVALANCHE Snow doesn't exactly move the same way water does, but there are similarities. If an avalanche breaks loose underfoot, use skiing (or even surfing) moves to try to ride on top of the snow, and attempt to get to the edge of the avalanche. If the snow is moving slowly, try to catch hold of a tree without getting crushed against it. In a fast-moving slide that knocks you off your feet, your best bet is to "swim" in the snow and try to avoid hitting any stationary objects.

IF YOU'RE BURIED ALIVE Being buried under the snow is not fun, but it doesn't have to be fatal. Once the snow in an avalanche flow stops moving, it turns from a fluid medium to a cement-like substance. Work quickly to dig your way to the surface as the slide slows. If possible, shove one arm

CAN'T DO WITHOUT

AVALANCHE BEACON An avalanche beacon is an indispensable piece of gear if you're crazy enough to spend time in areas with unstable snow. Turn the unit on, set it to transmit, and strap it around your waist and over a shoulder, under your outer layer of clothing. As always, let others know your plans prior to heading out. Now if you end up buried in the snow, rescuers can pick up your signal and know where to start digging.

upward and move it around to create an air shaft. Use your hands to carve out a breathing space. Work methodically so as to avoid exhaustion. Conserve your breath by waiting to shout until you hear rescuers above you.

PREDICT A MUDSLIDE Mudslides occur when sloping ground becomes so saturated with water that the soil loses its grip and gravity takes over. Then you get to deal with a filthy deluge that can destroy your property and put your life at risk. Be smart and observe the warning signs.

First and foremost, mudslides happen in places where they've happened before. Contact local authorities to learn the geographical history of your area, including any fires that have destroyed vegetation (which often leads to soil erosion) or construction that has altered water flow.

Always remember to avoid sharp inclines. Steep slopes that are close to the edge of a mountain range or valleys are

YOU MAY BE ABLE TO DIG YOURSELF OUT IF YOU KNOW WHICH WAY IS UP. IF YOU CAN SEE LIGHT SHINING THROUGH, GO THAT WAY. IF YOU'RE TOO DEEP, CLEAR A SPACE NEAR YOUR MOUTH AND SPIT. WATCH FOR WHICH WAY THE SPIT FALLS, AND HEAD THE OTHER WAY.

CAUGHT IN A ROCK SLIDE? USE SOME FAST FOOTWORK TO STAY ON TOP OF THE ROCKS, AND ATTEMPT TO MOVE TOWARD THE EDGE. IF YOU'RE BELOW THE TREE LINE OF THE MOUNTAIN, GET BEHIND A STOUT TREE SO THAT IT TAKES THE BRUNT OF THE IMPACT.

bad news. If your home is situated in a frequently hit spot, you might want to seriously consider moving.

Another thing to watch for is any changes in the patterns of storm-water drainage on slopes. If there's a river or stream nearby, sudden changes in water level—or a change in color from clear to brown—could indicate an impending slide. In addition, if you see cracks in the pavement, or walls pulling away from buildings, these are indications that the land is moving—which means it may be vulnerable to mudslides. This is also true if cracks appear in your house's foundation, or if doors and windows start to stick in their frames. Finally, keep an eye out for crooked stuff. Trees or telephone poles that are starting to lean aren't charming quirks. They mean the soil is eroding, and you should watch out.

SURVIVE A MUDSLIDE Mudslides can be spawned by earthquakes, volcanic eruptions, storms that dump a lot of water quickly, or just plain old erosion. However they start, they're pretty much always a dirty, bad time. Since most mudslide-related deaths occur at night, it's wise to have one person stay awake "on guard duty" when camping

YODELING CAN TRIGGER AN AVALANCHE

FALSE Despite what the movies have taught us, the act of yelling (or yodeling) in the snowy mountains usually doesn't trigger a slide. But a hard wipeout when you're skiing or snowboarding can, and it might start right beneath your feet. This self-activating doom is more likely to occur in unfrequented areas—not well-traveled ski trails. In addition to watching out for avalanche-prone areas, watch for triggers from other outdoor enthusiasts. Someone else falling upslope from your position can certainly activate an avalanche. And do try to keep your yelling and firecracker lighting to a minimum.

in a vulnerable area. If the rain is coming down hard and flooding and slides are predicted, put on a pot of coffee and continue to monitor weather and evacuation reports.

Listening for any rumbling sounds can also be a lifesaver. These massive amounts of soil, water, and debris don't just come crashing down silently. If you hear an ominous rumbling emanating from up the hill, get out of the area immediately. If there isn't enough time to evacuate, do the best you can to move out of the slide's way. If it's too late for that, curl into a tight ball and fold your arms over your head for protection.

AVOID A ROCKSLIDE Any hilly or mountainous areas with loose rock can be a site for rockslides. Recent rainfall, freezing and thawing, and seismic activity can all act as triggers for this '80s video game brought to life. Whether solitary rocks come rolling down the mountain, or an entire patch of loose scree starts sliding, get out of Dodge and seek cover. Don't hide in low spots, where rocks can pile up. Get behind sturdy protection and stay there until you no longer hear anything moving.

DESERT WASTELAND

BAKING SUN. BURNING SANDS. PLANTS ARMORED IN NEEDLES. IMPOSSIBLE THIRST IS THE ONLY THING DRIVING YOU TO MOVE. THE RIVER ON YOUR MAP IS CLOSE, BUT AS YOU CREST THE BANK, YOU SEE IT'S BONE DRY. ONLY STONES FILL THE RIVERBED, NOT THE WATER YOU'RE DYING TO REACH.

The world's deserts are places of inhospitable beauty. The living things that fill their emptiness are designed to bite, poke, or sting. Everything seems to bear a needle, and it's desperately trying to stick you with it.

Even the desert itself can hurt you—it's like a sponge sucking the moisture from your constantly drying body. Though you need the same gear and survival skills to endure these environs, not all deserts are the same. Some are filled with shifting sand dunes and little that's alive. Others initially seem hostile, but actually contain rivers, lakes, and other surprising water sources, as well as abundant life. Each desert is different and poses its own challenges, yet there are commonalities between them.

These are places of little rainfall, wild temperature swings, and often dangerous flora and fauna. Where else could you die of heat exhaustion or hypothermia just 12 hours apart? Only the toughest plants and animals can survive there, and the toughest, luckiest, or best prepared of people.

PREPARE YOURSELF The desert is unlike any other terrain on the planet. Food is scarce and water can be even scarcer, if not downright impossible to find. In most deserts (whether cold and dry or hot and dry), the only essentials you are guaranteed are the essentials that you bring with you. The water you carry may be your only water, so treat it like your lifeline (because it is). You'll also need a strategy for staying warm when the temperature plummets each night— warm sleeping bags and outerwear are going to be necessary items. Think of your trip to the desert as a trip to the moon—you need to be self-sufficient and self-contained. In short, if you didn't bring it with you, you won't have it when you need it.

THE STATS

134°F (57°C) World record hottest temperature, set in Death Valley, California in 2012.

-4°F (-20°C) Average temperature of the coldest desert in the world: the McMurdo Dry Valleys, in Antarctica.

0.59 INCHES (15 MM) Average yearly rainfall in the Atacama Desert in Chile, the driest non-polar desert in the world.

33% Approximate percentage of the Earth's land surface that is covered by desert.

20% Percentage of deserts that are actually covered by sand.

12 Number of countries crossed by the Sahara Desert.

250,000 SQUARE MILES (650,000 KM²) Amount of land covered by the *Rub 'al Khali* or "Empty Quarter," the largest sandy desert in the world, located on the Arabian Peninsula.

MOVEMENT Moving through the desert can be risky, even when everything is going right. The hot daytime temperatures, shifting sands, and impossible-to-judge distances make for a dangerous combination. Desert travel is safest in a fully stocked off-road vehicle. You should have abundant water and supplies, extra fuel, spare parts and tools, and sand mats to get your vehicle out of soft sand if you get stuck. Should you suffer an irreparable breakdown, stay with the vehicle—it's easier for rescuers to spot, and it provides shade and nighttime shelter. If you end up on foot and have a light source, travel during the night to make use of the cooler temperatures. If you're without lighting, travel in the morning and evening as much as possible, staying aware of local terrain and animal hazards. You don't want to walk off a cliff in the dark, or wander through lion country at dusk (prime hunting time). When walking, travel at an easy pace to avoid unnecessary sweating and water loss. Take frequent breaks to avoid overheating. Whether it's day or night, carry a walking stick to feel your way in the gloom and as a means of defense against desert denizens.

DEHYDRATION A top killer in the desert, dehydration can happen very rapidly in arid conditions, especially if you're exerting yourself and a desiccating wind is blowing. The first line of defense is obvious: hydrate. Don't ration your water. The best place to store your H_2O is in your system, not in a canteen. Some experts say you shouldn't drink for the first 24 hours of an arid climate emergency, but this may leave you very dehydrated and minimize the benefits of the water you do finally drink. To limit dehydration, keep all of your skin covered with light-colored clothing. Cotton is an acceptable choice for daytime wear in hot deserts. The cotton fibers hold water and decrease evaporative water loss from your skin. Just make sure you have dry clothes to change into when the sun begins to drop, as damp cotton can accelerate hypothermia on frigid desert nights. Don't worry about the old tricks of sucking on stones or chewing gum to slake your thirst: just keep your mouth closed and breathe through your nose. Keeping your face covered will limit some of the moisture loss through your breath as well.

GOOD TO KNOW

SOLAR STILL If there's ambient moisture in the area (and you're able to cobble together the components from what you have on hand), you might be able to collect drinking water using a solar still. This simple system concentrates and gathers water through evaporation. To make one, dig a hole, and place your chosen collection container at the bottom. Then cover the hole with a piece of clear or milky plastic, weighted so that water collects in the center over the bottle. If you're extra fancy, you'll have some tubing you can use as a long straw.

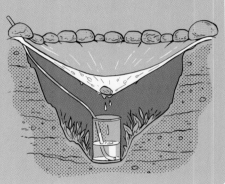

FINDING WATER Across much of the globe, drinking water can be sourced by simply walking downhill until a stream or creek is located. But water procurement can be a backwards business in some desert environments. Since the dry air and soils evaporate water along its normal downhill path, there are plenty of occasions when the nearest water is uphill, not downhill. You may follow riverbeds that come from seasonal flooding only to find the water course flattening out and disappearing altogether. Depending on the local geology, there may be pockets of water trapped on high ground and none down below. Try to gain some local information about the desert area's water sources before you begin any trek into arid country. It could also pay to bring along the sheet of clear plastic, shovel, and tubing necessary to make a solar still. Better yet, take a few extra gallons of water. Yep, I said "gallons," plural.

T / F

NEVER TRUST A MIRAGE

TRUE Full of hot air and disappointment, a mirage is an optical illusion. It's not a distant pool of rippling blue water as its appearance suggests. Mirage comes from the Latin root word *mirari*, which means "mirror." This strange yet common phenomenon happens when heat bends light rays, causing a water-like or mirrored reflection. There are many kinds of mirages, even rare, hard-to-see nighttime ones. But what isn't a mirage is vegetation. Bushes, trees, or ribbons of green in the distance can be indicators of a (real!) water source. There may not be much, and it may not even be at the surface, but if you're looking for a place to dig for water, vegetation can point the way.

SKILL

FIND SCARCE WATER A desert by definition must receive less than 10 inches (255 mm) of rain per year. This means that water is very hard to find, but you'll stand a better chance of survival with these tricks.

LOOK FOR LIFE If you see living creatures, there has to be water nearby. Look for flies, gnats, and bees, and see if you can spot where they're drinking. Birds may circle over bodies of water, so look skyward, too.

DIG A HOLE Desert plants grow from a source of groundwater. If you find a stand of vegetation in moist ground, dig at the roots and wait for water to seep into the hole.

GATHER DEW Wake up before sunrise and use a cotton shirt or towel to soak up dew from plants, or even rocks. Squeeze it into a container or straight into your mouth.

SURVIVE THE EXTREMES A land of shocking excesses and scarcity, deserts rarely have a "Goldilocks" zone where things are just right. Instead, these desolate tracts present a wide range of hazards from a number of extremes.

From the hot, dry, predator-rich grasslands of Africa to the cold, dry, lifeless mountain plateaus of the western Andes in South America, deserts are little used by humans, and with good reason. Survival in some areas may not be possible without significant preparation.

Bring tarps, space blankets, and rope to construct sun blocking shelters. Dig to create a depression at your shelter site, so you can lie on the cooler soil below. Face the shelter opening toward the north in the Northern Hemisphere and toward the south in the Southern Hemisphere to keep the midday sun from shining into your shanty. And don't try to build the full shelter or dig depressions in the heat of the day—wait until it cools down to do your work.

LOCATING FOOD Scrounging up some nourishment can be one of the most difficult tasks you'll face in the desert. With the lack of water comes a natural deficit in plant resources. When both of these are low, animal populations tend to be scant, as well.

Unless you're a foraging prodigy, the animal kingdom will provide your safest and least thorn-covered menu options. Not all creatures are edible, even after cooking (I'm talking to you, Gila monster). But with most beasts, you can remove all of their poisonous parts (such as a scorpion's stinger or a snake's head), cook until well done, and enjoy as a delicacy. Just make sure you don't let your guard down in areas inhabited by man-eating creatures—you don't want to end up on the menu yourself.

DIY SHADE Any shade is good shade in a sun-scorched area, but the best shade is the portable kind. You won't get very far on your journey if you're stuck hanging out under the only shade tree in sight. Instead, get crafty: stretch a space blanket or a piece of cloth over a branch to create a makeshift parasol. This allows you to walk and bring your "shade tree" with you wherever you go. More substantial

A Very Long Walk

Could you survive if you were lost in the Sahara Desert? Mauro Prosperi did. This Italian police officer and marathon runner became famous after his near-fatal detour in the Sahara during an endurance race in 1994. Prosperi ran the Marathon des Sables (Marathon of the Sands) in Morocco in 1994. A few days into the six-day-long, 145-mile (233-km) event, a sandstorm caused him to begin running off course. Disoriented and going the wrong way, he made it well into Algeria before he finally consumed all his food and ran out of water. He found shelter in an abandoned mosque, drank urine for hydration (a risky gambit—don't try it at home), and ate bats and snakes for sustenance. At a low point, Prosperi attempted to kill himself by cutting his wrists. But due to the severe dehydration, his blood was so thick that it clotted immediately. After nine days, a family of nomads found Prosperi close to death and brought him back to civilization. He had run an unbelievable 186 miles (299 km) off course, and had lost 40 pounds (18 kg). Not one to give up, Prosperi re-entered the same race in 1998 and again in 2012. He won in 2012, completing the course in 36 hours.

DRINK YOUR OWN URINE TO AVOID DEHYDRATION

FALSE Every survival class, I'm asked if drinking pee is an acceptable practice. Let's put a stop to that. The answer is no. If anyone's stuck in the desert and so dehydrated that urine is on the radar as a beverage – then the urine will be too concentrated to be a practical drink. Pee is full of waste products, and it leaves the body for a good reason. Drinking urine may keep you alive an extra day or two, but it costs the body some water to reprocess all the toxins that it just eliminated. Over time, this causes a net loss of water – not a gain. It's just basic pee economics, people.

CAN'T DO WITHOUT

SPACE BLANKET These reflective Mylar blankets are cheap, lightweight, and easy to carry. They can keep you warm at night and ward off the evil daytime sun. The blanket can be staked out on the ground as a ground-to-air signal panel, or you can cut a few strips off the edges and hang them up as trail markers. The blankets are waterproof, making for an ideal rain harvester. All you have to do is line a hole and wait for the skies to open up (which isn't that likely in the desert).

shelter can consist of tents or simple shelters made from tarps and rope. If these aren't available as building materials, then use brush and vegetation to build a brush hut—for shade and protection.

AVOID THE DESERT DWELLERS Nope, I'm not discouraging you from being friendly to people you meet in the dry lands. I'm suggesting that you avoid the animals of the desert, especially the snakes. It's easy enough to put away your boots and gloves at night (notorious spider and scorpion attractants), but avoiding snakes can be a trickier proposal. For starters, find a snake-proof shelter for your evening's rest. A tent or closed vehicle will do the job. If these aren't an option, do your best to tighten up any spots on your shelter where a snake could slither in, attracted to your generous body heat. Also, watch where you put your hands and feet during the daytime in snake-heavy areas. If you do get bitten by a venomous snake, follow these instructions: Cleanse the bite with soap and water (if available). Remove any jewelry on your hands and wrists, if the bite occurred near there. Immobilize the bitten area and, if possible, keep it lower than the heart. Cover the area with a clean, cool compress or a moist dressing to minimize swelling and discomfort. Monitor vital signs, such as temperature and pulse rate. Finally, if you can't reach emergency medical care within 30 minutes, place a suction device over the bite to help draw venom up out of the wound. Only use your mouth to suck out the venom as a last resort—and be sure to spit it out. Then wrap a bandage 2 to 4 inches (4 to 10 cm) above the bite to help slow the venom's movement. Don't totally cut off circulation—the bandage should be loose enough that you can slip a finger under it.

When it comes to scorpions, as with most of life's unpleasant circumstances, prevention is better than the cure. To keep from getting stung, be careful where you place your hands and where you sit or lie down when you're in scorpion territory. Be cautious when picking up anything that's been lying on the ground, including your sleeping bag and firewood. Before putting on clothing and footwear, shake them out to make sure nothing's inside, as scorpions love to hide in dark, cool places. If you do get stung, treat it like you would a snake bite, except for the venom sucking and the very real fear of dying. Scorpions stings are usually painful, but not life-threatening.

DESPITE YOUR NATURAL URGE TO BARE IT ALL IN THE HOT AND DESOLATE DESERT, KEEP YOUR SHIRT ON. THE MORE SKIN YOU HAVE COVERED, THE MORE YOU ARE PROTECTED FROM SUNBURN AND DEHYDRATION.

WILDFIRE

A FIRE OFFERS FRIENDLY WARMTH, BUT WHEN THE CONDITIONS ARE RIGHT, WIND, WEATHER, AND DRY VEGETATION CAN CONSPIRE TO TURN THAT FIRE INTO A HELLISH BLAZE. TERRIBLE TO BEHOLD AND RAVENOUS IN APPETITE, LITTLE CAN SURVIVE IN THE PATH OF THIS FIRESTORM.

For countless millennia, wildfires have been a natural part of ecosystems around the globe. These purging blazes clear away the dead grass and fallen branches. They turn vegetation into nourishing ash, and clear the way for new plant growth and regeneration.

In the natural system, these fires happen at intervals, contained in small areas without assistance, and the resident animals can flee to safety. But over the last century, more and more humans have begun living close to (or in the midst of) fire-prone areas. And as humans are able to stop most natural fires before they spread, the deadfall wood and flammable undergrowth can build to dangerous levels. So now, when a brush fire coincides with the right wind and weather patterns, all hell breaks loose. A wildfire of epic proportions erupts, severely damaging the environment and consuming homes and lives. There are few compromises to be found in the face of this modern problem: People need places to live, and some places need fire to live.

CAUGHT IN YOUR CAR One of the worst places to be trapped during a wildfire is inside a vehicle. It's still preferable to no shelter at all, but the radiant heat can turn the vehicle's metal exterior and small volume of air into a multi-person oven. If you do get caught in your car, roll up windows and close all vents. Park as far away from trees as possible, preferably next to a brick, block, or stone wall for partial protection. Turn off the engine, lie on the floor, and cover yourself with something. Don't leave your vehicle or try to run away on foot. The fastest runners are slowpokes compared to a raging fire. In some tragic cases, people tried to flee in their cars and drove right into the path of the fire. Follow evacuation orders closely, and never drive into the inferno.

334,200 Number of wildland fires that local fire departments in the U.S. respond to annually.

1 IN 5 Ratio of wildfires that are intentionally caused by humans.

37,000 SQUARE MILES (96,000 KM²) Area of land affected by the largest recorded wildfire in history, the Kalimantan and East Sumatra forest fires lasting from 1997–1998.

572°F (300°C) Ignition temperature of wood.

2,192°F (1,200°C) Temperature a forest fire can reach; in some extreme cases, temperatures can be even hotter.

1,000 FEET (300 M) Height that a forest fire's flames can reach; hot air currents can even create "fire tornadoes" that stretch this tall.

14 MPH (23 KPH) Speed of a wildfire on grasslands.

PREVENT A WILDFIRE Smokey the Bear doesn't like it when your campfire gets away from you—especially if it torches his forest home. The best way to fight a wildfire is to make sure you never start one.

If you're camping and you need a fire, pick a spot that has been used before. The safest spot to build a fire is in an existing fire pit, as surrounding flammable materials will already have been burned. If there isn't an existing campfire ring, then start from scratch. Look for a site that's at least 15 feet (5 m) from bushes, dry grasses, and other flammable objects. Avoid overhead foliage, too. Clear a spot 10 feet (3 m) in diameter, removing twigs, leaves, and anything else that can burn. Dig a pit in the soil about a foot (30 cm) deep. Circle the pit with rocks collected from a dry location, since waterlogged rocks may explode.

When you're done with the fire, pour water on it and stab the ashes repeatedly with a stick to allow the water to penetrate deeply.

KNOW THE CONDITIONS Wildfires can happen in a variety of environments. Dry, breezy grasslands, scrub-filled deserts, and drought-stricken evergreen forests are all likely candidates. Wildfires are also more likely in certain seasons. Regions that have a dry season and places with a lot of dead vegetation in autumn are seasonal hot spots for fires. These cycles of fire and regrowth are generally part of the area's natural life cycle. In fact, some plant species actually need the heat of a fire for growth and reproduction, though massive wildfires may be too hot, killing the fire-tolerant flora.

Since we are not fireproof like these hardy plants, keep some lifesaving tips in mind in case you get caught amidst a raging wildfire. For one, avoid canyons and other natural chimneys, as their natural wind flow patterns could draw in a fire and trap you. If possible, get into a river, lake, or other body of water, and lie back, using a wet piece of clothing over your face as both a heat shield and a smoke filter.

Make your way to breaks in the trees, which could mean breaks in the fuel—and therefore the fire. And if you're near a road, lie face down in a ditch or depression alongside it,

or get under the road if you can squeeze into a culvert or drainpipe. Whatever you do, cover up with anything that provides a shield against the heat.

FOLLOW THE WIND If you do get caught near a wildfire, remember that the most dangerous places to be are uphill from the fire and downwind from the flames. Let the wind point you in the safest direction of travel. If it's blowing toward the fire from your position, then run into the wind. But if the wind is behind the fire, blowing toward you, run on a course that's perpendicular to the wind, and move fast! That fire will be coming at you quickly.

FIGHT OR FLIGHT Some homeowners take a kind of Wild West approach to fire safety, ignoring evacuation orders in the face of a wildfire in order to stay and defend their homes. The common wisdom is not just to follow evacuation orders but, in fact, to get out early if it looks like the situation might become dire. However, the home-defense advocates point out that it's not uncommon for a home to burn to the ground as a result of just a few embers

IF YOU'RE CAUGHT OUT IN THE OPEN, MOVE TO AN AREA THAT HAS ALREADY BURNED. THIS MAY SEEM COUNTER-INTUITIVE, BUT THAT AREA HAS ALREADY HAD MOST OF ITS EASY FUEL CONSUMED. IT'S NOT LIKELY TO BURN AGAIN.

≈≈≈≈ T / F ≈≈≈≈

A WILDFIRE CAN MAKE ITS OWN WIND, FANNING ITS OWN FLAMES

TRUE A huge wildfire releases a massive amount of heat. As this heat rises, it pulls in cooler air below. This means that a certain size of wildfire can create its own wind. With self-generated winds, it becomes a true firestorm with widespread in-drafts (places where fresh air feeds into the fire) and a tall column of smoke and flame. Firestorms can also contain dangerous gusts and cyclonic swirls resembling fiery dust devils. These fires often occupy dozens of acres, with frightening intensity and runaway growth potential.

landing in dangerous spots like woodpiles, debris-laden gutters, or on foliage-covered rooftops. If someone had been there, they say, those fires could have been put out with a single bucket of water. But is it worth risking your life for a house and belongings? I say no. Pay your insurance and hit the road early, before people start driving crazily because they see flames in the rearview mirror.

SHELTER IN YOUR HOME If told to evacuate, do so. But if you're trapped at home, stay inside where the structure will protect you. Move to a central room, away from exterior walls. Close the doors to cut down on air circulation, which can feed flames. Place large plastic trash cans or buckets around the outside of the house and fill them with water, and make sure garden hoses can be directed into the house if needed. Soak burlap sacks, small rugs, and large rags; these can be helpful in beating out burning embers or small fires. Inside the house, fill bathtubs, sinks, and other containers with water. Water from toilet tanks and water heaters can also be used to battle any breakthrough flames.

FIRESCAPE FOR SAFETY The best offense is a good defense: in this case, that means "firescaping," a form of landscaping designed to keep your house from going up in smoke. Start by choosing the right kind of trees to plant. Conifers contain flammable and sometimes explosive oils and resins. Trees with broad leaves are usually a safer bet. Protect structures with fire-resistant, high-moisture vegetation like ice plants. Use a drip-irrigation system to water trees and shrubs year-round, or use non-flammable ground cover such as gravel.

Also make sure to maintain the trees within 30 feet (9 m) of your home by trimming dead or low-hanging branches, which will be the first to light up. While you're keeping dry wood away from the house, make sure your woodpile is off at a distance, too, and remember to cover external vents of your home with a fine mesh screen to keep embers from blowing in. You can even consider installing chimney caps, which keep embers from a wildfire out, and those from your fireplace in.

Oakland Hills Firestorm

*T*he Oakland Hills Firestorm was an unusual wildfire in that it happened in a densely populated area. By the time it was over, thousands of homes had been lost, and $1.5 billion in damage done. The fire began as a roadside grass fire on Saturday, October 19. Local firefighters thought they'd extinguished it, but it reignited on Sunday morning, October 20, and quickly became a major threat to the California cities of Oakland and Berkeley. Winds of up to 70 mph (110 kph) fanned the blaze, and its heat was great enough that it began generating its own winds, tossing embers in all directions, including across an 8-lane freeway, expanding the fire's perimeter faster than firefighters could keep up with.

A number of factors worked against the firefighters who were streaming in from around the state. Not all of their equipment was compatible, and fire hydrants on the narrow, winding streets were often blocked by parked cars.

Finally, after 72 hours, the winds died down and the 107-alarm fire was brought under control. It had killed 25 people and injured 150 more, and destroyed 3,354 houses, as well as a number of apartment buildings and condos., over an area spanning 1,520 acres (6.2 km²).

SHARK ATTACK

AN ANCIENT TERROR FROM THE DEEP, ITS GNASHING TEETH FEED ON FLESH. ALWAYS HUNTING, NEVER FULL, SHARKS HAUNT THE SEA AND CAN MAKE MEAT OF US ALL. PART MISUNDERSTOOD ANIMAL AND PART KILLING MACHINE, HERE'S WHAT TO DO IF A SHARK SETS ITS SIGHTS ON YOU.

Though shark attacks are actually quite rare, these animals still inspire fear in ocean waters. Among almost 500 species of sharks, only three have been responsible for a double-digit number of fatal attacks on people in recent times. One is the great white, as you may have guessed; the other two species are the tiger and bull sharks. And while you're more likely to experience a car accident than be bitten by a shark, humans tend to be much more frightened of these deep-sea monsters than of our own automobiles. And who can blame us?

Although sharks have a relatively low bite force (in fact, most common breeds of dogs can bite "harder" than the average shark), and most shark attacks don't end in death for the victim, that doesn't mean that the results aren't gruesome. The size of a shark's mouth and the sharpness of its serrated teeth make it easy for sharks to wreak havoc and create carnage, tearing off human limbs by simply clamping onto them and giving a quick thrash.

SKIP FEEDING TIME The time of day has always been a factor in the likelihood of a shark attack on humans. Dusk, nighttime, and dawn are the most popular feeding and hunting times for sharks. Of course, an attack can happen at any hour of the day or night, but nighttime and its transitions are statistically the worst times to be in the water. Many believe that the lack of visibility during these hours makes it easier for sharks to mistake you for one of their typical prey animals. Murky waters can play a similar role in these cases of tragically mistaken identity. So, while of course you really shouldn't hit the waves at all if a shark alert is called, to be extra safe only swim in potentially dangerous waters when the sun is high.

THE STATS

75 Number of shark attacks reported yearly worldwide.

60 MILLION Number of sharks killed yearly by humans, compared to an average of 20 annual human fatalities due to shark attacks.

99% Percentage of shark attacks attributed to only three species: the bull shark, the tiger shark, and the great white shark.

1,300 LBS (600 KG) Bite force of an average bull shark, the strongest of any living shark species.

11 FEET (3.3 M) Width of the jaws of the prehistoric Megalodon, the largest shark species to ever exist.

2,664 LBS (1,208 KG) Weight of the largest shark ever caught, a great white in Australia in 1959.

60 MPH (97 KPH) Top speed of a mako, the fastest shark species.

40 TO 1 Likelihood of drowning in Hawai'i vs. being attacked by a shark.

Sharks don't usually hunt people as a food source, which is why most shark bites stop there . . . as a bite. Once the shark realizes you're not a nice fat seal, it leaves you alone. Unfortunately, that little "mistake" isn't all that little for the human on the receiving end of those chompers. At the end of the day, shark attacks are basically an odds game based on how many hours you spend in the water. But there are a few ways to stack the deck in your favor.

KNOW SHARK HOTSPOTS While sharks are open-ocean predators, most shark encounters are in the shallows and near food sources. The best warning sign for shark attack activity is an actual sign that says "WARNING: Shark Attack Activity." But if the sign makers have been slacking in that area, there are other things to watch out for. For one, avoid river mouths and channels. These are places where dead animals and fish wash out into the ocean. This intersection of waterways is usually a popular feeding area for sharks, and it's even more dangerous after it rains. The water becomes murky, and low visibility makes it harder for sharks to identify their prey. Other hotspots include areas with dead animals and fish, fishing activity, sewage dumping into the ocean (lots of reasons to avoid those spots), underwater drop-offs, and sandbars. Coral reefs are popular shark hangouts, too—and also happen to be the most desirable dive sites.

BE UNATTRACTIVE You don't need to dump a canister of shark repellent (a real thing) into the sea when you take a dip, but it helps to be less attractive as a target. Since sharks tend to attack individuals, make sure to swim, dive, or surf in groups and take advantage of strength in numbers. Don't wear swimwear or wetsuits that are bright or high-contrasting in color, and leave the shiny jewelry at home. Garb in bright colors such as yellow and orange may attract sharks, and shiny jewelry may resemble the scales of a fish. Also, watch your movements. Playfully splashing around in water can attract sharks, as it resembles their prey in distress. And even if you are actually in distress, avoid erratic movements and splashing.

GOOD TO KNOW

Sharks aren't the only animal of the deep that can pose a danger to humans. There are plenty of other dodgy creatures in the sea.

BLUE-RINGED OCTOPUS When disturbed, this colorful little killer may bite—and it has a neurotoxic venom which causes numbness, paralysis, and death from respiratory failure.

STINGRAYS Stingrays can lash out with their whip-like tails, equipped with one or two barbed spines. Beloved animal educator and celebrity Steve Irwin, aka "The Crocodile Hunter," died in 2006 from a stingray stabbing.

BARRACUDA The great barracuda has sharp, jagged teeth and strong, tearing jaws, and it has been known to attack swimmers in the Atlantic, Caribbean, and Pacific.

STONEFISH The stonefish looks like a rock on the seabed, and is occasionally stepped on in shallow waters. It has 13 venomous spines along its back, and victims suffer intense pain, paralysis, shock, and even death.

FLEE FOR YOUR LIFE If you see a fin pop up on the surface of the water, or you spy a shark in your vicinity, get out of there! If there is a shark sighting, regardless of how epic the waves are, get out of the water. Live to surf, swim, and dive another day. If you do suddenly find yourself in close quarters with one of these beasts, your best bet is still to

T/F

SHARKS CAN SMELL BLOOD IN THE WATER

TRUE You really don't want to keep surfing if you're bleeding, even a tiny bit, as you are potentially chumming the water with blood and attracting curious sharks. Most shark species have enough sensitivity to smell and taste your blood from over a mile (1.6 km) away. And that's not their most impressive trick. Like a bloodhound picking out one human scent from a crowd of different humans, sharks can track the blood scent back to you. Even though you are not a blubbery seal or walrus, your blood draws hunger. So if your surfboard hits you in the face and gives you a bloody nose or you just started your period, get out of sharky waters.

CARRY A DIVE KNIFE. WHETHER YOU NEED TO CUT YOURSELF FREE FROM AN ABANDONED NET OR FEND OFF A SHARK, A WELL-HONED AND CORROSION-RESISTANT DIVE KNIFE COULD MAKE THE DIFFERENCE BETWEEN LIFE AND DEATH.

try getting out of the water. Swim away with smooth, even strokes that won't attract attention. You won't be able to outswim a shark, but maybe you can stay off its radar. One other trick, suited to divers, is to submerge and hide. Divers have reported successful evasion by descending to the seafloor and waiting for the sharks to leave. But that only works if you've got an air tank.

STAY AFLOAT Your sea kayak, lift raft, or dinghy offers a surprising amount of protection from inquisitive sharks. A shark may bump it with its nose, to investigate this strange floating object, but you are usually safe within the craft's protective embrace. When one or more sharks are present in the water, it's probably the right time to paddle somewhere else—or get a bigger boat.

FACE YOUR FOE When a shark wants to eat you, you'll know in advance: It will hunch its back, lower its fins, and rush at you in a zigzag pattern. Thrust your spear gun, camera housing, knife, or whatever else you're packing to discourage it. If the only thing you have is your surfboard, use it as a shield to create a barrier against the shark. Who cares if it takes a few bites—better the board than your torso. If you are swimming and completely unarmed, punch the shark's supersensitive nose, or stab at its eyes or gills. If the shark bites into you and begins to drag you underwater, don't play dead or give up. Get aggressive and do some damage to the shark. It may just let go.

STOP THE BLEEDING If you do get bitten by a shark, get out of the water as quickly and as efficiently as you can. Once a shark realizes that you are not its usual high-fat prey animal, it typically lets go. The numbers don't lie. Shark attack fatalities are usually from blood loss and injuries sustained in the attack, not from being eaten. With blood loss as your most life-threatening issue, get out of the water quickly, as it will prevent your wounds from clotting. Apply direct pressure on the wounds, tie tourniquets on limbs (if necessary), and get help immediately. Immediate medical attention is the best way to avoid a fatality.

Jaws of Death

*I*t was a hot summer day in 1963, and Rodney Fox was competing in a spearfishing contest off the Australia coast. After about four hours, Fox was dissatisfied with his catch, and decided to swim out farther and deeper than the other competitors. He'd gotten quite a ways from shore when he felt something slam into his chest. "I thought I'd been hit by a train, of all things," he recalled. But then he saw the teeth.

Knowing that a shark's eyes are sensitive, he attempted to gouge at them. That seemed to work—the shark let go, and he fell out of its mouth. Unfortunately, his arm ripped open on the shark's teeth as he dropped. He realized the shark had him deep underwater, and he broke for the surface. The shark followed him, and yanked him down by his float line. In an amazing series of coincidences, the shark bit through the line, allowing him to surface again just as a boat came by to check on the source of blood in the water.

Fox was rushed to a hospital, where it took doctors 462 stitches to put him back together. He went on to invent and promote the concept of shark-cage diving and consulted on a little movie called *Jaws*.

TROUBLE AFLOAT

OCEAN IN EVERY DIRECTION, AND THE ONLY SOUND IS THE WATER, SLAPPING YOUR DERELICT BOAT'S HULL. THE MOTOR WENT, AND WITH IT, YOUR WAY OUT OF THIS MADDENING EXPANSE OF BLUE WATER. WILL YOUR PATH CROSS THAT OF ANOTHER SHIP BEFORE YOU DIE OF THIRST?

A ship can be many things to many people. It is a means of conveyance, taking people and goods from one point to another. It is a vehicle for discovery and a means for adventure on the water. It can even be a vacation destination, loaded with luxuries and decadence.

Whatever the purpose, the craft is a protective environment that keeps you insulated and safe from the dangers and hardships of the sea—that is, when everything is going right. But when things start going wrong, the vessel begins to feel less like a cocoon of protection and more like a floating prison, trapping you in a hostile environment and leaving you at the mercy of the ocean.

During an emergency aboard a boat or ship, your options for survival can be limited, especially if you cannot get away. Yet even today, when most of the world's travelers make their way by automobile, train, or airplane, the nautical world still sings a siren's song, luring people out onto the frightening and fascinating seas.

SEND AN SOS For almost 100 years, SOS was the standard international distress signal for ships. This set of three letters in Morse code is a sequence of three dots, three dashes, and three dots (··· – – – ···). It has often been associated with phrases like "save our ship," "send out succor," and "save our souls," but in truth, it doesn't actually stand for anything. This nine-element signal remained the chief maritime radio distress signal until 1999, when it was replaced by the Global Maritime Distress and Safety System. The GMDSS is an automated system that can transmit GPS information and automatic distress calls, as well as a number of other types of data. The old Morse code sequence is still recognized worldwide, if it comes to that.

THE STATS

5,500 MILES (8,851 KM) Longest survival record at sea, set by three Mexican fishermen adrift 285 days; two of the original five died before being rescued.

$120 MILLION Annual value of goods lost in Somali pirate attacks.

1 BILLION GALLONS (3.78 BILLION LITERS) Amount of sewage dumped by cruise ships annually.

4,386 Number of fatalities from the collision of the ferry *Doña Paz* and the oil tanker *MT Vector* in the Philippines in 1987.

THE MATRIX

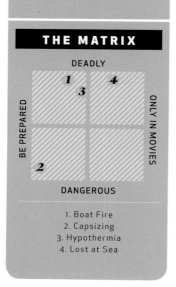

DEADLY

BE PREPARED

ONLY IN MOVIES

DANGEROUS

1. Boat Fire
2. Capsizing
3. Hypothermia
4. Lost at Sea

SHIP'S AFLAME A fire onboard your boat is a life-threatening event. And since you can't exactly run away from it, you need a firefighting plan in place before you leave shore. Always store fresh fire extinguishers in locations near the galley and the engine compartment, which are the two most likely locations for fire. If fire breaks out, move everyone out of the cabin and get them into life vests. Call VHF channel 16 to report the emergency, and prepare to abandon ship. Fight the fire with extinguishers, keeping a clear escape route behind you at all times. Remember to always aim fire extinguishers at the base of the fire.

BOTTOMS UP Small boats capsize easily, but they're easy to right. Crawl up onto the overturned hull, grab the centerboard (keel), and lean back, using your weight against the centerboard as a lever to flip the boat over. When it's upright, crawl aboard and bail out the water.

If your capsized boat is a motorboat without a centerboard, righting it will take a bit more doing. Tie one end of a rope to something secure in the middle of the boat, like an oarlock. Toss the free end of the rope up onto the hull. Crawl onto the hull to grab the free end of the rope, facing the side where the rope is tied. Back up toward the water and lean back, using your weight against the rope to pull the boat over. Then scramble aboard and start bailing.

PATCH THINGS TOGETHER Ever had that sinking feeling? I assure you, it's much worse when you're on the water. Collecting water inside the boat is often inevitable due to rain or waves coming over the bow. These aren't big issues—but when you've sprung a leak, the boat can sink in a hurry.

Your top priority is to find the trouble spot and locate the leak. If you can't find it, head for dry land quickly. Always check to see that the boat's drain plug is closed—it's a common culprit for leaks.

Once you find the leak, you may be able to do your own mending. If the leak is caused by a failed thru-hull fitting, stop it with a conical soft-wood plug that should be tethered to the hull. If the hull is fractured due to impact,

SKILL

Even tropical waters can conduct away your body heat, killing you via hypothermia. Here's how to stay warm and stay alive.

GET OUT If you're in the water, get out immediately. If your boat has capsized, right it, then bail the water.

STAY TOGETHER If stranded with a group, cling together for warmth. Face inward, hold on tight, and tread water.

HELP YOURSELF If you're wearing a life vest, assume the heat escape lessening posture (HELP): draw your legs up, fold your arms across your chest, and keep your face out of the water.

STAY STILL Don't swim, as that circulates cold water around you.

place a large plastic sheet across the leak on the outside. Secure the plastic with ropes, and water pressure will help hold it in place as you carefully head for land.

ABANDON SHIP! Even if you're the captain, you don't want to go down with a sinking boat. When it's time to abandon ship, move as fast as you can. You want to be away from the crowd to avoid jostling for position. Move to the railing and prepare to jump. If the ship is rolling to one side, abandon ship from the high side so you aren't crushed by the boat if it capsizes. If you're higher than 15 feet (5 m) above the water, it's too dangerous. Find a lower position or wait for the ship to sink further. Cross your arms over your chest and grab your lapels (or the area where they'd be). This position protects your neck and shoulders so that when you hit the water they don't break. Look for a spot in the water that's free of debris and aim for it. It will take some

---

T/F

SEAWATER CAN DRIVE YOU CRAZY

TRUE Brain chemistry is a fragile thing, and when coupled with dehydration, drinking salt water can lead to dangerous hallucinations and actions. In 1982, a yacht named *Trashman* sank in the Atlantic, leaving the five-person crew adrift in a life raft. One crewmember died of her injuries early in the ordeal, and two others began drinking seawater against the captain's orders. Soon after, one of them became convinced that his car was nearby and jumped into the water. He was killed almost immediately by the sharks circling the raft. A short time later, the other man declared that he was going out for cigarettes and swam away, only to be lost at sea.

SKILL

START A FLOODED MOTOR Boat motors are complex machines, but you don't have to be a mechanical genius to get one running again, especially if a flooded motor is the reason you're stranded at sea.

STEP ONE Remove any spark plugs and wipe them dry.

STEP TWO Crank the motor several times to blow excess fuel out of the combustion chamber.

STEP THREE Reinstall the spark plugs and then reconnect the wires.

STEP FOUR Raise the warm-up or fast-idle lever and crank the starter no more than 8 to 10 seconds before pausing.

STEP FIVE If the motor doesn't start, crank the starter again.

STEP SIX After the engine starts, leave the fast-idle lever up until the motor runs smoothly and you should be good to go.

courage, but when you've picked your spot, don't wait. As you leave the rail, cross your feet at the ankles—keeping your legs together will help prevent the force of the impact from causing injury. Take a big breath just before the splash. The biggest danger of being close to a sinking ship is getting clobbered by debris falling from the deck, so get yourself well out of the way. It's also difficult to swim in the turbulent water around a sinking vessel. Swim at least 100 feet (30 m) from the ship. Use either a sidestroke or a backstroke to conserve energy, while keeping your eyes peeled for obstacles or hazards.

WHEN THE WATER'S ON FIRE In an event where you must swim through burning fuel or oil, the irony of the situation runs deep. Stay under the surface too long and you'll drown; come up too soon or in the wrong spot and you'll inhale only flames. If your ship goes under, oil tanks can rupture, releasing fuel that covers the surface of the water. If that film ignites—and when a ship sinks, it almost always does—you have to get through it to safety. Follow a few simple but important steps, starting with jumping feet-first through the flames. Submerge and swim beneath the surface, but don't try to hold your breath for too long, as that tends to cause panic. When you come up for air, try to look for a clear area. Keep your arms extended over your head, and violently splash the surface with your hands as you emerge to throw the burning oil clear. Take your breath, then immediately dive again. Repeat the process until you're clear. If injury prevents you from swimming underwater, swim at the surface while constantly splashing the oil away from you on all sides.

SIGNAL OTHER CRAFT Signaling for help is your best chance to get to safety. The most effective signaling device is an emergency position-indicating radio beacon (EPIRB), which notifies rescuers via a global satellite system. The next best device is a very-high-frequency (VHF) or single-sideband (SSB) radio. When making a mayday call, calmly and clearly state your GPS coordinates, the nature of your emergency, a description of your vessel, and the number of

people on board. Once you believe rescue is close at hand, use visual signals like aerial flares, smoke, and dye markers. Don't shoot a flare unless you know someone is close enough to see it, and aim it over the water so you don't risk setting your boat on fire. In daylight, use a signal mirror, flashing it at the horizon.

STAY ALIVE Once you've made it to the lifeboat, your work is far from over. Now the monotonous tasks of open water survival take over. You'll have to catch food, collect safe water, and deal with any other issues that arise.

When it comes to food, I hope you like fish. If you're in a life raft, small fish often gather beneath the raft, either out of curiosity or because they feel sheltered there. Catching your own sushi is not only a great pastime, but it's also your primary source of nourishment. Troll a hand line with a hook and anything flashy that can serve as a lure. Try moving the lure up and down, at different depths below the surface. But be incredibly careful not to snag the life raft with the hook. After catching your first fish, use its guts as bait to catch more fish.

The issue of drinking water is paramount—all that water, and none safe to drink? This is yet another ironic part of water survival. You'll need to be prepared, resourceful, and willing to work hard if you expect to collect enough drinkable water. Prepare yourself by outfitting your vessel

EAT WHAT YOU MUST. ADRIFT SURVIVORS HAVE MADE MEALS OUT OF RAW FISH, RAW SEA BIRD, RAW TURTLE, AND ANYTHING ELSE THAT THEY WERE ABLE TO CATCH WITH HOOKS OR THEIR BARE HANDS. DON'T BE SQUEAMISH IF YOU WANT TO LIVE.

T / F

YOUR PANTS CAN BE USED FOR FLOTATION

TRUE Many clothing items can function as temporary emergency floatation devices, assuming the cloth is woven tightly enough to trap air inside it. While treading water, wriggle out of your pants, making sure you don't lose them in the water. Tie an overhand knot in the cuff of each leg to seal it off. Flip the waist of the pants out of the water quickly, to scoop air in. Squeeze the waist closed and place an air-filled pant leg under each arm. Catch your breath and enjoy your brief stay in a higher position out of the water. Repeat often, and get creative, using sleeves and other garments to make air pockets.

SKILL

MAKE SHIFT HOOKS Since you can't exactly go foraging for food when you're adrift (unless you have a hankering for some seaweed), you need a way to bring the food to you—namely, fishing gear. Fishing line and hooks have also been used to patch holes in rafts and to catch birds and turtles. Pack a variety of hook and line sizes to catch both little fish and big ones. Or, if worst comes to worst, you can improvise a hook from a safety pin, soda-can pull-tab, or other items. It's much smarter to have a survival fishing kit handy.

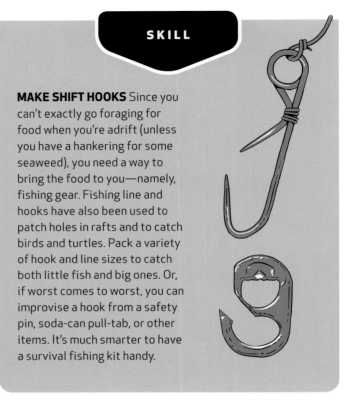

with a plastic tarp and some containers. You can use the tarp to catch rainwater and fill the containers. If you end up without the tarp, be resourceful by using any fabric you have to absorb moisture, then wring it out into containers. If you have sails, make a bowl out of them to capture the water. Tarps, shirts, plastic sheets, and even the raft itself can all collect water. Any can, bottle, or other container can store it. When you've been adrift at sea for a period of time, all your clothes end up encrusted with salt crystals. At the first sign of rain, give all your clothes and other fabric a seawater bath. Yes, it's salty, but not as salty as the salt residue, which will make any water it contacts undrinkable. The first water you collect will have a high salt content, so store it separately, and use it to clean wounds or to wash food before eating. Never drink saltwater—it will make you ill and speed dehydration and death.

Life on a Raft

One of the most amazing tales of survival at sea is the story of Steve Callahan, who spent 76 days in a life raft in the Atlantic Ocean in 1982. The ordeal began when Callahan's 21.3-foot (6.5-m) sloop was badly damaged during a night storm off the Canary Islands. He sought refuge on a 6-person raft, with a just a few minimal supplies. As the raft drifted westward with the current, Callahan soon exhausted his food supplies and began living off fish and other aquatic animals. He primarily caught and consumed mahi-mahi and triggerfish, mixing it up with other fish, barnacles, and birds. During his 1,800-nautical-mile (3,300-km) trek across the ocean, he survived by drinking water from two solar stills and collecting rainwater, which averaged only a pint (0.5 L) of water per day.

On his 75th night adrift, Callahan saw the lights of Marie Galante Island. The next day, he was spotted by some fishermen and taken to a local hospital. He had lost a third of his body weight and was covered with sores, but he had survived—after two months lost at sea and near death from starvation and dehydration.

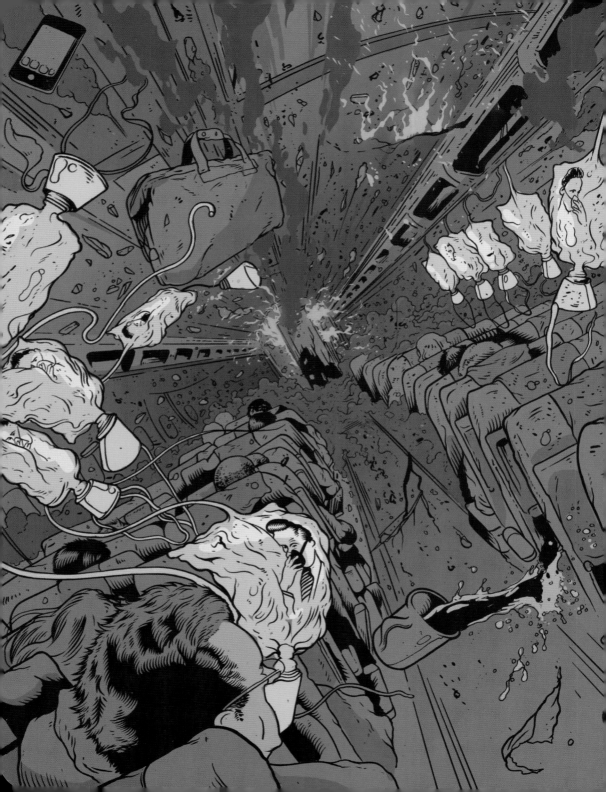

DEATH IN THE AIR

SCIENCE AND SKILLED PILOTING LIFT THESE METAL HULKS INTO THE AIR—
AND SET THEM BACK DOWN. THE PHYSICS IS BAFFLING, BUT THE FIGURES
DON'T LIE: FLYING IS GENERALLY SAFE. BUT GOOD ODDS GIVE LITTLE
COMFORT WHEN THE PLANE BEGINS TO HEAVE AND BUCK.

Plane crashes are exceedingly rare, but that knowledge is little comfort when you've had a few drinks, the lights are flickering, the seatbelt sign is definitely on, and you're white-knuckling it through a bumpy, turbulent flight. Despite the rarity of accidents involving aircraft, it's easy to fixate on the bad scenarios that we imagine–rather than remembering all the safe and successful flights we never paid any attention to. When things go wrong on a plane, it's usually very quick and unexpected.

Not surprisingly, the last words spoken before a plane crash often involve a hasty reference to a malfunction, a brief mention of God, a final quick message to a loved one, or an outburst of profanity. There aren't many lengthy explanations or long farewells, because there's not much time to react. That's why it's so important to know what's going on, what to do, and how to do it–so that you can react appropriately during a disaster and make the right moves. Your survival depends on it.

KEEP YOUR SEAT BELT FASTENED
This isn't just sound advice when traveling by automobile. Even though the captain may turn off the fasten seat belts sign and tell you that you're free to move about the cabin—don't. People have died from injuries sustained during aircraft turbulence, injuries that a seat belt would have prevented. Each year in the U.S., about 60 people are injured from failing to wear their seat belts in flight, and three people have died from these accidents since 1980. All it takes is one patch of clear-air turbulence to launch you out of your seat and slam your head against the ceiling above. Sure, you'll have to take the belt off if you need an in-flight bathroom break, but other than that, keep your seat belt on until the plane has stopped.

583 The record highest number of fatalities in an airline disaster, from a collision of airliners at Los Rodeos airport in Tenerife, Spain in 1977.

239 Number of missing persons from the 2014 disappearance of Malaysia Airlines Flight 370.

$1.4 BILLION Cost of the B-2 Stealth Bomber crash in Guam, in February 2008; the single most expensive aviation accident in history.

570 MPH (917 KPH) Average cruising speed of a Boeing 747 airliner.

1 IN 4.7 MILLION Odds of being killed in an airline accident.

33,333 FEET (10,160 M) Highest survived altitude of a human falling from an aircraft without a parachute; Vesna Vulović, a former Serbian flight attendant, was the only survivor of Yugoslav Airlines Flight 367 in 1972.

HOPE TO CRASH ON LAND There's a big difference between a water landing and an emergency landing on terra firma. That difference is survivability. Ditching into an ocean or lake may seem like a softer landing, and it may well be, but the secondary risks associated with water—drowning and hypothermia—make it more dangerous for its crashed passengers than crash landing on the ground. On land, you can run, walk, or crawl away from the plane. On water, you'll probably have nowhere to go.

ASSUME THE POSITION Research has proven that airplane brace positions do increase the chances of survival in an emergency crash landing. The basic positions are as follows: Keep your feet flat on the floor. Wear your seat belt low and tight over your lap. If the seat in front of you is close, place your head and hands against it. If there's too much room for that, bring your chest to your knees and grip your shins with your hands. Stay in either position until the plane has come to a stop.

These positions reduce the high velocity of your head when it inevitably slams into the seat in front of you. They also minimize limb flailing, thereby minimizing injury and increasing your chances of being whole and hale enough to escape the crashed plane. (Just imagine how hard it would be to unbuckle your seat belt with two broken arms, or climb over seats to the emergency exit with a broken leg.)

If you are headed for a water landing, be ready to use the flotation devices aboard and to grab and use the oxygen masks, should they be deployed. Since young children and infants cannot use the adult brace position, an adult should hold the child as tightly as they can with one arm, and continue their own brace position with their other arm. Teens and kids too big for the lap should assume the brace position and be buckled into their own seat.

USE YOUR CHUTE A parachute won't be an option when you're one of many on a commercial flight, but when it's just you and old Willy flying around in his biodiesel Cessna, having a parachute onboard is fairly standard, and can definitely be the thing that saves your life. If you decide it's

SCAVENGE A CRASH SITE After a plane crash, survivors must stay alive until rescue. With a little creativity, you can find plenty of useful items.

Check the cockpit radio. If it works, send out a distress call. Use the fuselage as a shelter—unless fuel has spilled, in which case there's a chance of fire; stay about 100 feet (30 m) away.

If the plane has broken up, use the carpeting, cushions, bulkheads, doors, and windows as shelter. Look for electrical wires to lash things together, and reflective materials for signaling.

Go through luggage to find clothing, blankets, pillows, food, and water. Also grab any eyeglasses or medications.

Advanced medical supplies, including automatic defibrillators, may be onboard. Don't leave those critical lifesaving items behind..

the right time to jump out of the airplane, then make sure you wear and use your parachute correctly.

To don your chute, step into the harness so the leg-hole straps encircle your thighs, then bring the top straps over your shoulders and tighten the harness across your chest. Don't touch the ripcord before exiting the plane. When you jump from the airplane, do it any way you can—except in front of an engine. If you think falling's bad, you should see what passing through a turbine will do to your day. After the jump, count to three, then pull the rip cord. As you float, plan your landing. Steer the parachute by pulling the

KNOW WHERE THE EXITS ARE AND BE ABLE TO FIND THEM EVEN IF YOU CANNOT SEE THEM. A CRASH MAY FILL THE CABIN WITH BLACK SMOKE, WHICH WOULD KEEP YOU FROM LOCATING YOUR NEAREST EXIT IN YOUR MOMENT OF NEED.

GOOD TO KNOW

KNOW YOUR SEAT The safest seats on the plane are the exit row seats above each wing and the aisle seats nearby. The exit row seats give you the first crack at getting out, and sitting in an aisle seat near the exit is good for those who tend to feel claustrophobic or those who want to get off the aircraft in a timely manner (emergency or not).

The worst seats on the plane are the window seats furthest from the exits. These seats away from the exits will require a longer trip out of the plane. The first few rows of seats can also be dicey—they're close to the front exit, which is a good thing, but they're also vulnerable to frontal impacts in a crash.

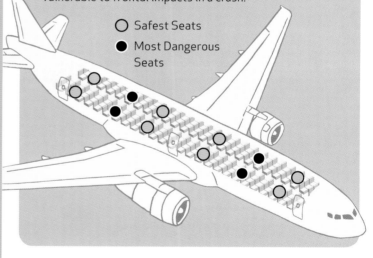

○ Safest Seats
● Most Dangerous Seats

handles, using the ones on your right to go right and those on your left to head left. Before landing, bend your knees, tuck in your elbows, and lower your chin to your chest. Roll with the landing.

STAY IN YOUR SEAT It's true that people have jumped out of planes without a chute and lived, but that's a poor flight plan, to say the least—especially considering the sudden stop at the end. In the event that your plane explodes or comes apart in midair, stay in your seat. On Christmas Eve 1971, teenager Juliane Koepcke survived after falling about 10,000 feet (3 km), still strapped to her seat, before crashing through the rainforest canopy and coming to rest on the forest floor in Peru. Although several others survived the midair breakup and long fall as she had, Koepcke was the only one who survived being lost in the jungle after the crash of LANSA Flight 508.

CALL FOR HELP You aren't supposed to make calls on a cell phone during a commercial flight, because electromagnetic interference from the phone might adversely affect aircraft controls. However, if you can't reach the cockpit to use the radio—or if the radio's down—all bets are off. (That was certainly the case on September 11, 2001, when passengers on United Airlines flight 93 placed emergency calls after terrorists took control of the plane.) As long as there's a cell tower in range, a mobile phone will work on a plane. The lower the plane's altitude, the greater the chances for a successful connection—and for getting assistance.

FIGHT BACK A hijacking is a nightmare scenario to be sure, and you can bet that your hijackers don't have any nice plans for you. Should you be on one of these ill-fated flights, do everything in your power to fight back against the hijackers. You'll have to be resourceful, using improvised weapons and attacking by surprise to retake control of the plane. If the hijackers are pilots, as they were on 9/11, then the rightful pilots may be dead. It's still worth trying to retake the plane, and it's the right thing to do. If you prevail, get on the radio and place your mayday call on the frequency that's already set, since that's likely to be the one the local tower uses. If you need to select a frequency, try 121.5 MHz or 243.0 MHz, which air-traffic control usually monitors. The vast majority of successful landings by non-pilots are assisted by air-traffic controllers. Many are pilots themselves, so they're likely to know how to get you down safely.

T / F
YOU CAN TAKE SURVIVAL GEAR ON A PLANE

TRUE If you want to be prepared for anything, you might want to pack some TSA-compliant survival gear in your carry-on luggage. Your flight-friendly survival pack can include one book of safety matches per person, dental floss, a compass, a metal cup, paracord bracelets or bootlaces, a hydration bladder (empty), and a small flashlight. Keep in mind that you can't bring any kind of blade or knife, butane lighters, strike-anywhere matches, lighter fluid, torch-style lighters, camping stoves, tools, MREs with a heater accessory, and anything else that could potentially be used as a weapon or to start a fire on the flight.

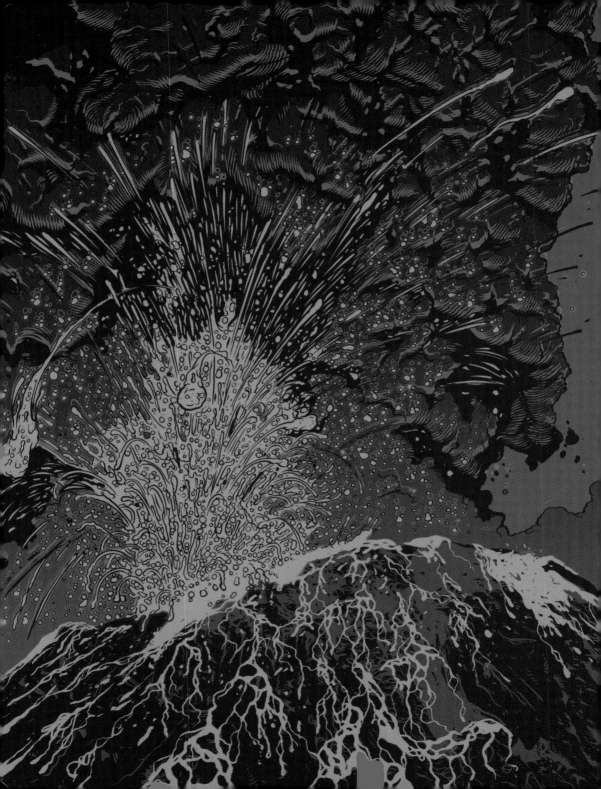

FIRE IN THE SKY

THE MOUNTAIN RUMBLES, SMOKES, AND GLOWS. WE ARE NO LESS FRIGHTENED BY THIS VOLCANIC UPHEAVAL THAN OUR ANCESTORS WERE. THE MOUNTAIN IS TRYING TO KILL US WITH LAVA, ASH, AND FUMES. WITHOUT THE RIGHT SHELTER, WE MIGHT AS WELL BE IN A MUD HUT IN POMPEII.

You may think of volcanoes as exotic things, with beautiful, slow-moving lava streams and gnarly, twisted rock formations you can visit on faraway holidays. This is especially the case for people living outside the "ring of fire." But the inhabitants of the volcanically active Pacific Rim know better.

Volcanoes are geology in progress—the quick kind that can level entire regions or build new mountains in a matter of days. Volcanoes also wield fearful weapons like poisonous gases, incinerating lava, and deadly pyroclastic flows. And volcanic activity isn't confined to the Pacific Ocean perimeter. Volcanic mountains in other parts of the world can erupt at any time. One good eruption from the supervolcano that slumbers under Yellowstone Park could change life in the United States for generations to come.

Volcanoes build the land, forming islands in the sea and making rich, fertile soil, but they can also wreak havoc, particularly for those who live near them.

SHELTER IN YOUR CAR A car isn't going to give you much protection from the fumes and ash of a volcano, but being inside a vehicle is much better than standing outside in the ash fall. If you take refuge from a volcanic eruption in a vehicle, keep your engine turned off and make sure all windows are tightly shut. Use tape, if you have any handy, to seal any accessible vents. If you have to drive (to flee the area, for example), avoid doing so while the ash is falling heavily. Driving in this fine ash dust will quickly clog your air filter—and your engine. Also remember never to operate the air conditioning system in these situations. Running the AC will bring in outside air—and the ash and fumes that come with it.

THE STATS

2,982 MILES (4,800 KM) Distance from which the 1883 Krakatoa blast could be heard; the blast shattered victims' eardrums 40 miles (64 km) from the volcano.

7 Number of times that the echo of Krakatoa's eruption circled around the world.

2,200°F (1,200°C) Average temperature of volcanic lava.

3,000 Estimated minimum number of living humans remaining worldwide after the Toba Catastrophe, a supervolcanic eruption in Indonesia in approximately 75,000 B.C.E.

670 MPH (1,080 KPH) Fastest pyroclastic flow (hot gases and mineral ash ejected during an eruption) down a volcanic slope; recorded during the 1980 Mt. Saint Helens eruption.

33,474 FEET (10,203 M) Height of Mauna Kea from its base at the ocean floor to its peak; the volcano's total height is greater than that of Mt. Everest.

When the earth blows its top, the dangers include fiery lava bombs lobbed by the eruption, a tide of molten rock, and the toxic fumes of pyroclastic gas flows.

GET ON THE ROAD The best place to be is far away. Distance is the best protection against the hellfire and fury of a volcano, so be ready to evacuate when the warning is issued. Get out before the ash starts falling, because your vehicle may stall out during the ash fall, leaving you in a worse predicament than if you'd stayed home.

SHELTER AT HOME If you can't put space between you and the eruption, find shelter and cross your fingers. A house can provide protection from ash and falling debris, but then again, it could catch on fire. So if you shelter inside, be ready to hustle out fast. During ash fall, stay inside, especially if you have a respiratory ailment. Close doors, windows, vents, and chimney flues. Turn off all fans and heating and air conditioning systems. Monitor radio and TV broadcasts about the situation. The flow will head downhill, so wherever you hole up, make sure it's not in a low-lying area.

COPE WITH ASH OUTDOORS Volcanic ash is far from soft and fluffy. It's composed of tiny, jagged pieces of rock and glass—hard, abrasive, and corrosive. Because it destroys engines when it's sucked into the intake, volcanic ash can halt ground transportation for hundreds of miles (or kilometers) around an eruption, and divert air traffic for thousands. But if you live close to an active volcano, your problems might be more immediate. If you get caught outdoors during an eruption, take every precaution to protect your skin, lungs, and eyes.

When outside, put on layers; wear long sleeves and pants to protect your skin from ash. Breathe through a dust mask, or at least hold a damp cloth over your nose and mouth. The razor-sharp pieces in the ash can slice up your lungs and lead to permanent respiratory impairment. And dust masks may not be enough; even a top-quality particulate respirator (dust mask) will not filter out toxic gases and

vapors. Sulfur gases, methane, carbon monoxide, and numerous other toxic gases are common expulsions from volcanoes. Finally, make sure to protect your eyes; use goggles or wear eyeglasses instead of contact lenses.

ASSESS A LAVA FIELD Even if you're pretty sure it has cooled and hardened, it's better to detour around a lava field—because if you're wrong, you're toast. Almost literally. If you must cross, tread lightly. Try to ensure that the lava has totally hardened. You can't always tell by looking, because molten lava might be flowing below a thin crust that can fool you. As you make your way forward, probe the ground ahead with a stick. Pay attention to air quality, as sulfur dioxide gases indicate flowing lava beneath you. This gives you two reasons to get away: Not only is the ground unstable, but the gas is toxic. If the soles of your boots start to melt, the flow is too hot to cross. And if the ground feels at all mushy, that means it's too unstable to hold weight.

THE INVISIBLE POISONOUS GASES THAT FLOW FROM A VOLCANO MOVE A LOT FASTER THAN THE LAVA THAT IS VISIBLE. IF A VOLCANO STARTS UP NEAR YOU, STAY SAFER BY GOING UPWIND AND AVOIDING LOW AREAS.

THE EARTH MOVES

THE PHRASE "AS SOLID AS THE GROUND BENEATH YOUR FEET" MEANS NOTHING WHEN THE GROUND OPENS UP. EARTHQUAKES CAN HAPPEN ANYWHERE, ANYTIME, AND BEING PREPARED PLAYS A MAJOR ROLE IN SURVIVING THE CALAMITY OF A QUAKE.

*I*t's easy to think that earthquakes only affect specific areas of the world, but in reality, the majority of the earth is vulnerable to seismic instability. Just because some regions rarely experience earthquakes doesn't mean that they can't happen—even on a massive scale. Californians, Alaskans, and Hawaiians have been bracing for "the big one" for decades, but people in other parts of the world may find themselves dangerously underprepared for the damage that a major earthquake can deliver.

A great example of a jolt from nowhere is the August 23, 2011 5.8 magnitude earthquake in eastern Virginia. I was teaching a survival class that afternoon in a forested patch of land 30 miles (48 km) from the quake's epicenter, which was near the town of Mineral, Virginia. The ground rumbled like thunder, the trees shook furiously, and branches started crashing to the ground all around us. We ran like scared jackrabbits to reach a safer clearing where nothing could fall on us.

UNEXPECTED LOCATIONS The east coast has never been known as a hotbed of earthquake activity, but the 6.0 magnitude earthquake in Cape Ann, Massachusetts on November 18, 1755 was strong enough to be felt all the way from Nova Scotia down to the Chesapeake Bay in Maryland. The sparse population and heavy timber building techniques of the colonial era prevented any fatalities, but nearly 1,600 chimneys were knocked down, several brick walls collapsed, and in some areas near Boston, cracks opened in the ground. Those aboard a ship sailing near Cape Ann felt the shock and thought they had run aground. Had this quake occurred in modern times, the property damage and loss of life would have been great.

PREPARE FOR THE WORST If you live in an earthquake-prone area (or even if you don't), it's never a bad idea to take precautions against such events. Purchase a utility shut-off wrench, and keep it in a handy place. Make sure there is nothing heavy that can fall on any of the beds in your home. Bolt or strap bookcases, shelving units, and water heaters to the wall studs behind them. Give your home a walkthrough, considering what could fall and how to prevent it. One final idea is to avoid glass jars and bottles for your emergency food and water storage. How awful would it be to store plenty of food and water for your family, and then find only a soggy heap of spoiling food and broken glass after an earthquake?

WHAT TO DO WHEN IT HITS A surprising number of people—including those in quake-prone regions, who should take a keen interest in the topic—don't know what to do when the shaking starts. But a little foresight could save your life.

First, know how to take cover. Assess every room you spend time in and pick the spot that's likely to be safest in a quake. For instance, if your office has a sturdy desk, you might want to follow the classic "duck, cover, and hold" advice by diving under the desk and holding on to its legs. Stay there until the shaking stops.

Avoid windows. They may seem like a way out of danger, especially since you can see through them, but just imagine the damage that big broken pieces of glass can do to the human body. Glass moves and breaks in strange patterns during earthquakes, and these broken pieces can be deadly if they fall on you—or you fall onto them.

If there's nothing sturdy enough to protect you from falling rubble (which could include fragments of the ceiling), use the "triangle of life" tactic (see sidebar, page 134). Crouch beside a large, stable piece of furniture that could deflect debris. Or cover your face and head, and stoop in an inside corner of the building that's away from possible falling objects.

Never hide under the bed. The small space underneath will be made even smaller if the ceiling collapses on it. If you are in bed during the night and an earthquake occurs,

simply roll off the bed and stay near the edge. The bed will hold up some of the debris, creating a safe void around the perimeter of the bed. Never get under it, and teach your children never to crawl under the bed in an earthquake.

Also steer clear of the stairs. The average stairway is a deathtrap in an earthquake. The treads can cut a person into pieces if the building collapses on top of them. Don't be on or under the stairs during a quake.

Finally, if you're outside when a quake hits, head to an open space that's away from structures, streetlights, and overhead wires. The area of highest risk is directly outside any buildings.

RIDE OUT AN EARTHQUAKE IN A CAR You probably know the drill: If you're inside a building when an earthquake hits, stay there. If you're outside, get into a clearing. But what if you're driving? The first thing to do is to stop

T / F
A DOORWAY IS A SAFE HAVEN DURING AN EARTHQUAKE

FALSE Despite what you've heard over the years, standing in a doorway during a quake is actually a terrible strategy. The idea likely stemmed from people's knowledge of the extra wooden studs in the wall around the doorway. While these studs do hold up a considerable amount of weight, they cannot make up for the actual hole in the wall that a doorway represents. If you are in a doorway and the door jamb falls forward or backward, you will still get crushed by the ceiling. And people have actually been cut in half by a collapsed doorway, when the jamb falls horizontally. In any event, don't stay under doorways in a quake!

TRIANGLE OF LIFE So where should you go if you're caught indoors during an earthquake? Many search and rescue professionals advise seeking the "triangle of life." This concept involves the triangular voids that solid objects create amid earthquake debris. Imagine a ceiling falling in—people who hunker down next to desks and couches are often saved because the objects take the brunt of the weight. Being under the desk may seem more logical—and if the desk can handle the weight, go for it—but it can in fact be more dangerous if not made of sturdy materials. If you're not sure, it's safer next to the desk—because even if the desk is completely crushed, the ceiling will still be partially supported. If you're lucky, you'll be crouched in the void—with enough space to survive.

driving if you are in a relatively safe spot (not on a bridge or under an overpass). There are two main hazards during an earthquake on the road: other drivers and falling objects. Pull over in an area where hazards such as telephone poles, street lights, and, yes, even overpasses are unlikely to fall on your car. The more open the area, the safer it is. If you are unlucky enough to be on a bridge when the quake hits, take the next exit off it—pronto. And if you're stuck under an overpass with no way to exit, get out of your car and lie flat beside it. If the structure collapses, it will definitely crush your car, but usually not all the way to the ground. Hopefully, the car's body will leave a safe zone immediately surrounding the vehicle. Once the earthquake has stopped, there may be aftershocks, so don't hurry off. Listen to the radio for updates that may affect your route, and remember to expect accidents and damage all around you.

SURVIVE BEING TRAPPED UNDER DEBRIS See a clear path to safety? Then get yourself out. But if the walls come down and you're inside, find ways to help others get you out—people trapped inside usually can't save themselves. Let rescuers know where you are by tapping on a pipe or wall. Use a whistle if you have one. To avoid inhaling dust, cover your mouth and nose with a cloth, and use your voice only as a last resort. Don't light a match or lighter to see where you are, as there could easily be a gas leak.

TAKE ACTION AFTER AN EARTHQUAKE Surviving the shake doesn't mean you're out of the woods. What you do immediately after an earthquake is just as important as what you do during one. Fire prevention should be the top item on your post-disaster to-do list. If the building you're in appears to be structurally sound, open doors and windows to ventilate gas fumes or dust. Avoid using any gas or electrical appliances, since the greatest danger after an earthquake is fire. It's also wise to put on boots or shoes with heavy soles, long pants, and a pair of sturdy gloves before you go running out into the street. These will help you avoid injury from sharp objects. In addition, rubberized gloves can block potential electrical hazards.

GOOD TO KNOW

MEASURING MAGNITUDE Seismologists use the Richter scale to quantify the energy released by earthquakes across the globe. The power of these massive seismic shifts can compare to the force of a lightning bolt or an atomic bomb, all the way up to the massive Krakatoa.

Magnitude	Comparison (left)	Number	Comparison (right)
9		<1	Krakatoa Eruption
8	Mount St Helens Eruption	1	World's Largest Nuclear Test
7		18	
6		150	Hiroshima Atomic Bomb
5		1,500	Average Tornado
4		10,000	Lightning Bolt
3		100,000	
2		1,000,000	

NUMBER OF EARTHQUAKES A YEAR

4 SMALLEST EARTHQUAKE FELT BY HUMANS		**5** LIGHT PROPERTY DAMAGE	
6 MODERATE PROPERTY DAMAGE		**7** MAJOR PROPERTY DAMAGE, LOSS OF LIFE	
8 SEVERE ECONOMIC IMPACT, LARGE LOSS OF LIFE		**9** WIDESPREAD DEATH AND DESTRUCTION	

MAKE SURE YOU KNOW WHERE GAS AND WATER SHUT-OFFS ARE LOCATED IN YOUR HOME AND BUSINESS. KEEP THE NECESSARY TOOLS NEAR THE SHUT-OFFS SO THAT YOU CAN TURN THEM OFF QUICKLY IN THE EVENT OF EARTHQUAKE DAMAGE TO THE LINES.

HOME INVASION

YOUR HOME IS YOUR CASTLE, PLACE OF REFUGE, AND SAFETY FROM THE WORLD OUTSIDE. BUT THAT SECURITY CAN COMPLETELY DISAPPEAR WHEN THE CASTLE IS BREACHED AND ROBBERS BREAK IN TO THREATEN YOUR FAMILY. WHAT CAN YOU DO WHEN THE BAD GUYS GET IN?

Statistically speaking, the chances of a home invasion are pretty slim. This is a rare event in the civilized world, and your odds of being involved are low—that is, of course, unless you live in a rough part of town, or if you have a stash of valuables (and the habit of talking about them in public).

But although your odds may be low, break-ins do happen frequently, and if we look at the data in a different way—say, the number of robberies in your locality—they will tell you a different story. Even in seemingly low-crime areas, the number of break-ins and robberies can be shocking, and sometimes a simple B & E (breaking and entering) can escalate into something much, much worse.

The likelihood of this unwelcome entry depends on the attractiveness of your home to robbery, the crime rates in the area, and the preventive measures you take to make your home a less tempting target. And if the crooks pick your house, it's important to know what to do and when to do it to avoid being at the mercy of villains.

FIGHT OR FLIGHT? It's been said that discretion is the better part of valor. Put more plainly, caution is more important than blind bravery—and there's no shame in running away if running away is going to save your life. But fleeing won't always be the best course of action. For example, you yourself may be capable of running away, but you may have a mobility-impaired family member who cannot escape. So how do you determine whether you should fight or flee in a home invasion scenario? It's simple: If all members of your household are able to flee the home, and you have an opportunity, then do so. But if any members of your family cannot get away, then it might be time to try to scare the criminals away.

THE STATS

1 IN 5 Ratio of homes that are burglarized at some point in their existence.

ONCE EVERY 15 SECONDS Rate at which burglaries occur in the U.S.

1.9 MILLION Number of residential burglaries in the U.S. in 2013.

59% Percentage of home invasions that involve forcible entry.

$2,200 Average financial loss per act of burglary committed in the U.S.

28% Percentage of burglaries committed while a household member was present.

65% Percentage of violent home invasions where the perpetrator was known to the victim.

7% Proportion of home-invasion robberies in which a resident experiences some form of violence or threat from the invader.

TAKE SECURITY SERIOUSLY Most home invasions start with envy—someone sees something that he or she wants, and then plans to steal it. Take the following common-sense precautions: First, make your home a less appealing target. Keep valuables in secure locations— such as bank lockboxes—instead of home safes or hiding places. Remember not to discuss your valuables and material possessions with others. For in-home repairs, use only licensed, reputable workers, and always check their identification. If you can, install motion-activated lights on the exterior of your house, and always leave on a few lights while you're out. Keep all windows and doors locked, including garage doors. Opt for additional locking mechanisms, such as deadbolts or locking bars for sliding-glass doors. You can also wedge a broom handle behind sliding doors and windows for a budget option. And lastly, consider getting a guard dog. Or two.

EARLY WARNING Most burglars want to enter silently, burgle quietly, and then leave without a sound. This is why a loud alarm system is so important. This can be a commercial system that is professionally installed and monitored, or you can try your luck with some home-grown options.

For starters, you just can't beat a real, professionally installed security system. The door and window alarms, motion detectors, and other sensors for an in-home security system are the best—if the electricity is working. But you'll have to fall back to Plan B if the grid's down. If you don't want or can't afford a real security system, set up some outdoor motion sensor lights, or up the ante by connecting a sprinkler system to the same sensors. It's one thing to illuminate a burglar—just imagine his surprise when he's not only lit up but soaked, too. You can also place door chimes on the backs of all interior doors. If the door moves, the bell will let you know that something's up. Another (or additional) option is putting bells on door handles or window latches.

At the least, there's always the "do-nothing method." Don't repair squeaky floorboards or oil your door hinges. If

GOOD TO KNOW

You can't help marveling at the athleticism and coordination of stars like Jackie Chan, especially their stunts using everyday objects as weapons. While most of us will never have that kind of dexterity, we can take a page from Hollywood fiction and use household objects as very real, improvised weapons. Here are just a few ideas:

•Kitchen knives, cleavers, rolling pins, and other heavy, sharp, or pointy kitchen tools

•A tightly rolled-up magazine

•Hardcover books

•Chairs

•Pots and pans, particularly ones containing scalding-hot food or water

• Bookcases and shelving units (when pushed over onto your assailant)

•Pens and pencils

•A fire extinguisher or a fireplace poker

you know the third stair creaks when you step on it, leave it that way. These passive alarms are more effective than you may think. You'll get used to the noise on an everyday basis, but they'll grab your attention if they sound when they shouldn't. The best part? They won't cost you a dime.

AVOID CONFRONTATION People can get killed when they try to confront home invaders, particularly if the criminals feel cornered or trapped. Most places allow you to legally defend yourself in a home invasion, but you're on safer and more legally defensible ground if you try to retreat. Some of my law enforcement friends advise retreating to a fortified room in the event of a robbery. While moving there, announce "You are trespassing! Get out! I have called the

T / F

DON'T PLAY POSSUM DURING A HOME INVASION

TRUE One of the many responses to imminent peril is the act of freezing in place, just like the possum (which faints during attacks to feign being already dead). This may be the oldest trick in the book, but in modern times, it's not the right approach. Though it's possible the robbers will believe you're asleep and ignore you, you can never count on humanity from criminals. The majority of them are dangerous people. Always act as if your life is in danger. Call 911, arm yourself, retreat to a better protected spot, and be ready to put up a fight.

police! I am retreating away from you! If you come closer, it is because you mean to kill me!" If they keep coming after all that, then you have a right to worry, and to defend yourself with any weapons at your disposal.

DEFEND AGAINST A KNIFE ATTACK When you're facing an armed assailant, your goal is to escape injury and, above all, to stay alive. If an intruder does come at you with a knife, stay far enough back that your attacker can't slice you, then deploy the Nike defense: Run! If you can't escape, then your only recourse may be to try to disarm him. If things do reach that point, surprise your attacker with explosive violence. Grab the attacker's wrist, angle the blade away from yourself, and bash his hand over and over against a wall, a piece of furniture, or any other hard object until he drops the blade. Or you could bring a gun to the knife fight—that works, too.

WHAT IF YOU'RE TIED UP? Bound and tied by your home invaders? There are a few ways to unfetter yourself with materials at hand. If your wrists have been duct taped together, find a rough or sharp square edge and abrade the duct tape restraints until you've cut the tape. The edge of a door works great, and every room has at least one door. Zip ties are a little harder, but still achievable. The best two techniques to get free from zips are to violently break them or saw them with cordage. To break them, hold your bound hands up near your face. Then swing your elbows down and behind you as fast and as hard as you can. This will slam the zip ties against your belly, often straining the locking strip to its breaking point. Repeat harder if it doesn't work the first time, or try cutting the ties with cord. The cord cut is simple, but laborious. Untie your shoes or boots (hopefully you're wearing some) and remove the laces (this works well with paracord). Tie the loose laces together and tie a large loop on each end. Thread the cord through one zip tie. Place each foot in the two cord loops, and move your feet like you're pedaling a bike. This will saw the cord back and forth on the zip tie, heating it, melting it, and eventually breaking it.

CAN'T DO WITHOUT

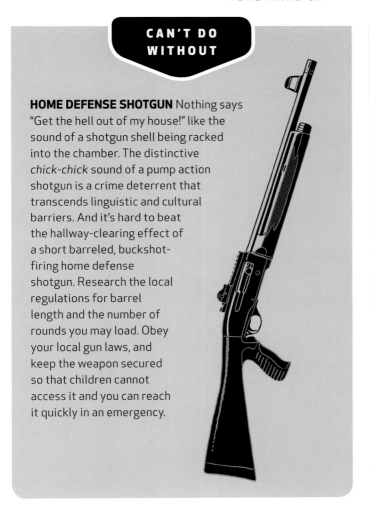

HOME DEFENSE SHOTGUN Nothing says "Get the hell out of my house!" like the sound of a shotgun shell being racked into the chamber. The distinctive *chick-chick* sound of a pump action shotgun is a crime deterrent that transcends linguistic and cultural barriers. And it's hard to beat the hallway-clearing effect of a short barreled, buckshot-firing home defense shotgun. Research the local regulations for barrel length and the number of rounds you may load. Obey your local gun laws, and keep the weapon secured so that children cannot access it and you can reach it quickly in an emergency.

DON'T CONTAMINATE THE CRIME SCENE Some of the recent advancements in forensics are absolute scientific wonders. The information that a fiber, a drop of blood, or a fingerprint yields can be used in court to lock up the bad guys for quite a while. If you are unfortunate enough to be embroiled in some type of robbery or break-in, make every effort to preserve the integrity of the crime scene. Leave things where they lie. Don't disturb anything that could be used as evidence. In fact, do yourself a favor and leave after the police are done with your statement.

IF YOU WERE A CRIMINAL, WOULD YOU ROB THE BRIGHTLY LIT DWELLING WITH ALARM STICKERS? OR THE DIMLY LIT ONE WITH AN OPEN WINDOW? LOOK AT YOUR HOUSE WITH NEW EYES, AND TAKE STEPS TO MAKE YOUR HOME A LESS ATTRACTIVE TARGET.

MOB RULE

THE MOOD CHANGES. THE CROWD GETS AGITATED. AS MORE PEOPLE REALIZE THAT THEY WON'T GET WHAT THEY WANT, THEY BEGIN TO LASH OUT. BOTTLES FLY, FIRES BLAZE, AND THE POLICE BEGIN TO MOVE IN. YOU'RE IN A DANGEROUS SITUATION WHEN A GATHERING TURNS INTO A RIOT.

What do you call it when a crowd takes on a collective consciousness of its own—and starts wrecking the place? Well, you'd call it a riot. And sometimes it seems that the bigger the crowd, the lower the mob's collective IQ score.

People may start out in the right— peacefully protesting a legitimate issue, for example—or for slightly stupider reasons, like an unfavorable (or favorable, inexplicably) sporting event outcome, but once the numbers swell, things usually take a bad turn. Cars start getting flipped over, businesses start getting looted, and fires start burning in the streets. To quell this violent uprising, the local law enforcement personnel have no choice but to move into the thick of it.

Riots are scary events, to be sure. But they are also survivable events, assuming you make the right moves. Regardless of where the riot is occurring or why people are upset, there are a few tricks you can use to get out of harm's way and ride out the storm of civil unrest.

DEAL WITH TEAR GAS Forget the various methods you'd use in a smokey fire, like wearing a wet bandanna over your face. Tear gas isn't smoke, so your makeshift breathing mask is not going to protect you from the deleterious effects of this popular crowd control method. Tear gas affects your breathing, coats your skin, and irritates your eyes. If you get sprayed or come into contact with a cloud of tear gas, leave the vicinity as quickly as possible, and try to breathe in short bursts through your nose. Avoid touching or rubbing your skin or eyes, which can cause chemical burns. Once out of the fray, use soapy water to wash away the tear gas and pour milk in your eyes if they're still irritated.

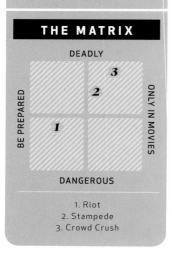
BE AWARE OF YOUR SURROUNDINGS Many people walk around blindly, playing with their phones and missing critical signs that can impact their well-being. The most basic urban survival skill is making sure you're not one of those people. Situational awareness is key to getting out of tricky scenarios—or, better yet, avoiding them entirely.

First, make sure to look around you. When you turn a corner or enter a crowd, watch out for potential dangers—and possible escape routes. Observe how other people are behaving, since their actions can clue you in to trouble spots you'll want to avoid. Second—and this may seem like odd advice—listen to rumors. Many will be false, of course, but information from credible sources can help you decide which people or places to avoid. Lastly, remember to use all your senses. Your nose can alert you to urban danger, like a fire in the street. You'll likely hear a commotion before you see it. And if something looks out of place, it is. Don't investigate. Get away.

STAY INFORMED Information is your best line of defense when dealing with a surly crowd. You'll need to find out the reasons for the riot, and you'll need to stay informed about where the situation is occurring.

Flipping on the television or your radio can provide you with some current local news, but that information can also be biased and outdated. The violence and size of a riot are sometimes downplayed by the authorities and media, in a logical effort to keep it from escalating with a fresh influx of rioters. For more information, you can also check social media. These outlets can sometimes provide local intel (though it can also be dead wrong, like most media). Whatever form of news you employ, use it to your advantage: Find out where the rioting is happening, and find out why.

STAY OFF THE RADAR The safest place to be in a riot is far away, but if you do get caught in one, it's best to blend in. Whatever issue has upset the people, just go with it. Chant the slogans that they chant, and repeat the types of things you're hearing around you. Don't stick up for the

SNIFFING STRONG ODORS CAN MINIMIZE THE EFFECTS OF TEAR GAS

FALSE Tear gas works because it's an outstanding irritant. It's hard to be unruly when you're in pain and you can't see or breathe. You might hear about an old Middle Eastern journalist trick of carrying a pungent onion in your pocket, ripping it open, and sniffing it deeply. Or you may hear that breathing through a rag soaked in vinegar or lemon juice will filter tear gas. But these homespun methods don't work against the highly effective and highly irritating RCAs (Riot Control Agents) used by modern military and law enforcement.

opposition unless you're trying to get a beating; tell them what they want to hear. If they have their faces covered, pull your undershirt up over your nose and blend in. But ditch the disguise as you reach the edge of the event—you don't need peaceful folks or law enforcement personnel getting the wrong idea about you.

SURVIVE A HUMAN STAMPEDE People react differently to panic. Some stand still. Others take off running and hollering. If you find yourself in a panicked crowd, you're at risk of getting trampled, so you'll need to act fast. Find some kind of substantial and immovable protection to hide behind: a large tree, a utility pole, a structural pillar, a wall, or a vehicle. Unless the mob is in full car-rollover-and-burn mode, you might even try taking refuge inside a vehicle until the masses have passed. If you do get trapped inside the stampede, stay on your feet and conserve your energy (don't resist the movement). Keep your arms and hands near your chest so you can create a little space around you.

It's a good idea to have an understanding of the crowd-control weapons law enforcement might use—and the hazards you might face from rioters.

BATONS AND SHIELDS Steer clear of the police so they don't mistake you for a rioter.

CONCUSSION GRENADES Hunker down and cover your head.

WATER CANNONS Hunch down so as not to get knocked off your feet.

RUBBER BULLETS Crouch and cover your face to avoid injury.

ROCKS AND BRICKS Duck and cover as you scramble to safety.

BOTTLES A missile that shatters is especially dangerous. Keep low and shield your eyes.

MOLOTOV COCKTAILS Run perpendicular to the cocktail's trajectory.

TEAR GAS Rioters may lob the canisters back toward police. Watch out!

Try to work your way diagonally toward the edge of the crowd. You'll be out of the worst of it and more likely to find a refuge or an escape route.

DEAL WITH AN INDOOR MOB Dealing with a panic-stricken crowd in tight quarters is a very dangerous scenario. A stadium riot, a concert stampede, or Black Friday can make for a lot of amped-up people in an enclosed space. If things get hostile, stay calm and look for an unorthodox exit that isn't packed with people. Businesses almost always have a back exit. But whatever you do, don't get pressed up against locked, stuck, or constricted doors. Frightened mobs have crushed people to death when the press of people pushed them against unyielding exits.

GET OUT OF DODGE If you find yourself in the middle of a riot, make your way to the edges where the press of people is thinner. Then find a course that leads you away from the angry crowd. Just make sure that your route is passable. Also be very careful not to get pushed up against a wall or fence where you could be trapped or even crushed by the press of the crowd. Find a safe and quiet spot to shelter, outside the area of rioting, and wait for the crowd die down. While waiting, if disturbances get louder or closer (or you smell smoke)—find a better place to hide.

STAY SAFE ON MASS TRANSIT In general, public transit is a good thing: It gets people around quickly and cheaply. But it does get a little dicey when the tight space of a bus, tram, or subway is full of people who are still in riot mode. To avoid a sticky situation, arm yourself with mass-transit know-how. First, know when your train or bus is scheduled to come. Arrive close to departure, cutting down on the time you spend lingering around stops or stations (near people who may be lingering for different reasons). This goes triple for night rides. Sometimes the closest station isn't the safest one. If it's poorly lit, poorly staffed, or a gathering spot for unsavory characters, walk to a safer transit hub. Again, this is very important at night. Once aboard, sit up front. Let the driver protect you.

Trampled in Tel Aviv

The story of how journalist Haggai Matar survived a Tel Aviv mob attack is a great (but scary) example of the speed and ferocity with which events can spin out of control.

In 2012, Matar had been writing stories about Africans who were seeking asylum in his home of south Tel Aviv. On May 23rd, in the evening, a fairly quiet demonstration turned violent when a young man threw Molotov cocktails into asylum seekers' homes. While witnessing this, Matar was approached by a woman who started screaming at him, thinking he was someone else. She cried out: "You throw stones at soldiers! Shame on you! Get the hell out of here!" Matar tried to verbally defend himself, denying the claim, but the woman's rant drew a crowd. She screamed again: "You lie! I see you every week on television throwing stones at soldiers and calling them Nazis!" One angry woman then became a group of ten people, and, within minutes, several dozen people had emerged from their homes. When people began beating Matar, he decided to run.

The mob followed after him until he reached the Hagana Bridge, which separates the greater part of Tel Aviv from its eastern neighborhoods. The police were at the bridge, which was a natural choke point for crowd control. Matar passed by them and safely returned home.

Others were not so lucky that evening, as the mob returned to the asylum seekers' businesses and homes, looting and attacking random people on the streets. Seventeen members of the mob were arrested, but the attacks went on for hours—well into the night.

THE GRID IS DOWN

THE FRIDGE IS FULL OF COLD BEER AND FROZEN FOOD. THE HOSPITAL IS FULL OF LIFE-SUPPORTING TECHNOLOGY. OUR COMPUTERS GIVE US ALL THE INFORMATION IN THE WORLD. AND IF THE ELECTRICAL GRID WENT DOWN, ALL OF THIS WOULD CEASE IN THE BLINK OF AN EYE.

We've all dealt with the annoyance of an electrical outage that lasted for a few hours, or perhaps even a few days. Maybe a thunderstorm knocked out the power, or maybe we forgot to pay the bill. Either way, our plugged-in home is now offline and inoperable. Our freezer lets the ice cream melt, the microwave stops cooking, and our TV has become a lifeless black screen, all due to the lack of electrical energy flowing to them. In rural areas, short outages are not uncommon. And in the wake of a disaster like Hurricanes Katrina or Sandy, the juice could be down for weeks. In these longer outages, civilization can unravel quickly, as spoiled and convenience-oriented people are forced to live a different kind of lifestyle. No electricity means little to no commerce, hampered medical care, limited travel, hindered communication, and a constant struggle for things like clean water and hot food. Most elements of our modern lifestyle would be severely crippled by a long and widespread grid failure.

WHAT ARE THE ODDS? Power grids are fragile systems, especially when damaged by a major disaster—or by successful hackers. They are also one of the most valuable systems of any nation, and are typically treated accordingly. Since electrical power is the energy source for most modern technology, it's far too valuable to lose. All threats to the grid are taken seriously, so chances are slim that something malicious could happen to it. That being said, most electrical grids are aging systems, full of expensive and hard-to-replace parts, and the demand for their power is continuously increasing due to a growing population and tech supply. Could it go down? Sure. Will it go down in your lifetime? Well . . . how lucky do you feel?

THE STATS

1 BILLION Number of people affected by the July 30th–31st blackouts in India in 2012, the largest power outage in history.

32 GIGAWATTS Estimated electrical capacity taken down during the above power outage.

2 MONTHS Duration of the power outages in Christchurch, New Zealand in 2011; 80% of the city lost power as the result of an earthquake.

48 HOURS Maximum time that a full freezer will safely hold food without power (refrigerators hold food safely up to 24 hours).

40°F (4.5°C) Temperature threshold above which refrigerated or frozen foods should be discarded.

1,037 Fires reported during the New York City blackout of 1977; this included 14 multiple-alarm fires.

3,776 People arrested in the 1977 New York blackout, the largest mass arrest in the city's history.

BASIC SURVIVAL The power's out, and your freezer is full of frozen food that is quickly becoming mush. What do you do after one day, three days, a week, or a month sans power?

Let's say you're listening to your battery-powered radio the day after an outage and you discover that it's not just you—the whole electrical grid is down. Eat your most perishable foods first (make a delicious meal with all the ice cream). The next meal can be frozen pizza cooked outdoors on a grill or by using a Dutch oven and briquettes. If you're hoping the power will be back any minute, go around the house to turn off or unplug all unnecessary or sensitive equipment (electric stove, computers, TV) so an electrical spike wouldn't damage them when the power is restored.

After three days without power, the fridge will be about empty, and you'll be dipping into the canned food and dry goods. Discard any questionable or potentially unsafe foods that have a foul odor, color, or texture. If you're lucky and in a residential area, your local water tower will probably still be working, so you'll still have drinking water—but for how long?

After one week, chances are good that municipal water and sewage services will be out. This means that you'll have to devise ways to collect and disinfect your drinking water. You'll also need to figure out how to make an outhouse—or at least a bucket toilet. The average household will also be running out of food, candles, batteries, and sanity by now.

After a month of living off the grid, the vast majority of unprepared people would be starving. You'd need to spend all of your time trying to beg, borrow, barter, or steal in order to get food. This length of crisis would make violent crime a common day job for many and reduce almost everyone to a hand-to-mouth existence. People living in the country on farms may seem to hold it together, but they would be under constant siege from marauders, beggars, and refugees.

TECH WORKAROUNDS The grid is the heart of the modern world, and electricity its lifeblood, but there are a few workarounds for short-term grid failure (or the first week of a long-term disaster) that can circumvent the modern

GOOD TO KNOW

THE ELECTRICAL GRID The grid is a complex and interconnected network that delivers electricity from the producers to the consumers. There are electrical generating stations that create the power, high-voltage transmission lines that carry the power, and distribution lines for the customers. There are three grids in the continental U.S.: east, west, and Texas.

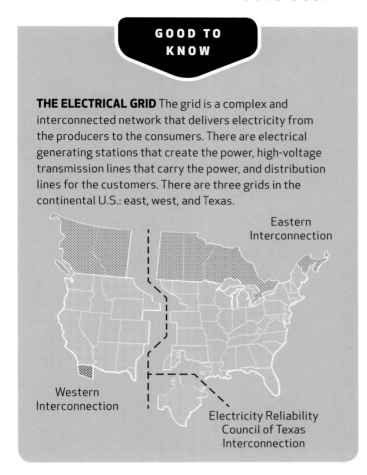

Eastern Interconnection

Western Interconnection

Electricity Reliability Council of Texas Interconnection

electrical grid. One of the most important things to have in a power outage event is a way to charge your cell phone; solar chargers are a nice investment, and AA-battery cell phone chargers are cheaper and more commonly available than solar. You can also use a car charger for devices—as long as the gas holds out. A larger, briefcase-sized solar panel will charge devices like phones and tablets, but not laptops. After a lengthy outage, cell phone towers probably won't be working, but a pricey satellite phone should still be operational, assuming you have someone to call who's as prepared as you are—in this crisis, and in whatever crisis may come your way next.

T/F

HACKERS COULD CRASH THE GRID AT ANYTIME

FALSE Though there are daily attempts to enter and damage the U.S. electrical grid's computer systems (from domestic hackers and outside agents), none are successful. Their agendas are diverse, and, thankfully, so are the methods that combat these unwelcome guests. The multitude of security specialists within the power companies and other organizations have successfully protected us since the birth of hacking. And let's hope they keep succeeding at their vital job—otherwise, we'll be bounced back to a *Little House on the Prairie* lifestyle—minus the civility and skills to be self-reliant.

THE UNTHINKABLE

Warning: Gloom and doom lie beyond this page. We saved the most outlandish and unthinkable scenarios for this final section. In essence, we saved the worst for last. This section is all about the long shots, the life-altering situations, and the system reboots. But make no mistake—this is not a video game. When you get killed, you can't just start the game over again. You only get one chance in this life, and this is it, right now. These grim scenarios deal with major emergencies and catastrophic events, which could happen anywhere and at any time. I truly hope none of us ever live to see them play out, but even in these troubling scenes of turmoil and hardship, there is a thread of hope. These disasters could be survivable—with the right combination of skill, preparation, and, yes, luck.

CONTAMINATED

IT ONLY TAKES A LITTLE HUMAN ERROR, OR A FAULTY MACHINE, TO UNLEASH POISONED AIR, TAINTED WATERS, OR DEADLY RADIATION. NO MATTER HOW AN INDUSTRIAL ACCIDENT HAPPENS IN OUR MODERN WORLD, THE RESULTS ARE STILL A TOXIC MESS—ONE THAT'S HARD TO CLEAN UP.

There are a multitude of ways that mistakes can occur in modern industry. Aging machinery may fail, an operator may fall asleep at the switch (sometimes literally!), or a natural disaster can trigger failures, as happened in 2011 when a tsunami caused a breach at the Fukushima nuclear plant in Japan. These incidents leaves us with a multitude of hazards that can harm those who live near the accident site. Whether it's a chemical plant that caught fire, a rail car of toxins that spilled, or a power plant meltdown, they all involve both immediate and long-term dangers.

For most industrial accidents, your survival strategies are the same: Shelter in place, seal up the windows, and wait for the "all-clear." But in some incidents (like an emergency at a nuclear power plant), your best bet is to grab your bug-out bag and flee. The more information you have the better. Add a little live local TV or radio to your daily routine, to stay in touch with what's going on in your area—just in case.

THE RULE OF THUMB Can one of your digits be a source of sound advice? Odd as it sounds, the answer is yes, at least in some circumstances. There is a common concept in emergency preparedness that if you can cover the source of trouble with your thumb when your arm is outstretched, then you are probably far enough away from the incident that you don't need to worry.

Of course, this test won't pan out 100 percent of the time, but as a general "rule of thumb," it means you are many miles away from the disturbance and likely out of danger. There are always exceptions, though. For example, if the issue is a cloud of toxic smoke and the prevailing winds are moving toward you, it's probably time to hit the road.

THE STATS

$200 BILLION Total cost of the 1986 Chernobyl incident, the worst nuclear disaster in history.

171,000 Number of people killed in the failure of the Banqiao Dam in Henan Province, China, in 1975.

558,000 People injured by the pesticide chemical leak from the Union Carbide plant in Bhopal, India in 1984, the worst industrial accident in history.

1962 The year the Centralia, Pennsylvania coal-mine fire started. It is still burning.

THE MATRIX

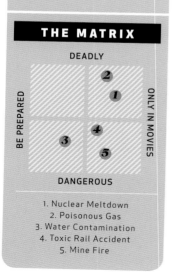

DEADLY

BE PREPARED

ONLY IN MOVIES

DANGEROUS

1. Nuclear Meltdown
2. Poisonous Gas
3. Water Contamination
4. Toxic Rail Accident
5. Mine Fire

WHEN A NUCLEAR PLANT FAILS How bad is bad? When there's a nuclear event, it's usually your safest bet to assume the worst. A breach may let out less radiation than an X-ray, but a full meltdown could blast you with enough radiation to kill within days. If all hell finally breaks loose and a the worst-case scenario occurs, you need to take cover. Immediately. The most important principle is to get as much mass between you and the radioactive dust and radiation as possible, since it can pass through walls and roofs. A onetime exposure to radiation is bad enough, but to make matters worse, this stuff can really stick around, for anywhere from eight days to more than a billion years, depending on the size of the incident.

In other words, if a radioactive event happens near you, know that you could be at risk long after the news coverage stops. The following strategies can help you deal with this kind of disaster.

First, think about shelter. Can you build a DIY bunker? If you have a basement, you're in luck. Pick the corner with the highest soil level outside, and push a heavy table into it. Then grab anything that's available and start heaping it on top—books, bricks, water containers, food stores, anything with high mass. Push large furniture up against all exposed sides of the table, leaving yourself a small entrance. Then get inside, seal it off, and wait it out, only coming out when absolutely necessary.

Next, remember that your local food and water sources are vulnerable to contamination. Animals are the most sensitive to exposure, and guess what: You're an animal. Chances are, you also eat animals and their products—such as beef, milk, and eggs. And many of those creatures eat grasses, which radioactive particles may coat. Avoid eating locally cultivated animal products following a nuclear event, especially if your government issues warnings. You may wish to stock up on potassium iodide tablets, which may prevent thyroid damage. It's best to purchase them prior to an emergency, as demand will quickly outstrip supply once it's too late.

Immediately after a nuclear event, authorities will be testing the local waters to see if they're safe to drink

CAN'T DO WITHOUT

RADIATION DETECTOR You don't need a full scale Geiger counter to measure radiation (though I wouldn't stop you from buying one if you lived downwind from and close to a power plant). There are other options to consider in radiation detection. Stickers and badges that change color in the presence of radiation are an affordable option, though not very precise. There are also small commercially available devices that can fit on a key chain, and alert you if you are in the vicinity of radiation. These can detect gamma and X-ray radiation and even beep at increased frequency to signal higher exposures.

or bathe in, and if fish and seafood is okay to eat. This is when that emergency water stock I've been talking about throughout this book is going to come in handy. Use it until you hear that the coast is clear.

Depending on the amount of exposure, land that has been impacted by radioactive fallout can suffer long-term damage, rendering it unusable for agriculture or residence for decades. Just because there's no radioactive material spewing into the atmosphere at the moment doesn't mean that it's safe to plant crops, raise livestock, or live in the area. Take, for instance, the land surrounding Chernobyl. It's still uninhabitable, more than twenty-five years after the nuclear accident that devastated the region.

T / F

PLASTIC SHEETING AND DUCT TAPE CAN SAVE YOU

TRUE Unlikely as it seems, these humble heroes can seal you off from some of the hazardous effects of an industrial accident. They won't turn your home into a hermetically sealed chamber, but they can help to reduce the volume of airborne particles infiltrating your house. Most homes have a great deal of air moving through the cracks around windows and doors. That's why it's so hard to heat a home in the winter and cool it in the summer. Sealing up these openings can significantly reduce the air movement, thereby reducing airborne contaminants. The tighter the seal, the safer you'll be.

SADLY, THE FIRST IMPULSE FROM BIG INDUSTRY, AND SOMETIMES EVEN LOCAL GOVERNMENT, IS TO DENY ANYTHING IS WRONG. IF YOUR WATER TASTES FUNNY (OR BURSTS INTO FLAMES!), GO INTO SURVIVAL MODE NO MATTER WHAT YOU'RE TOLD.

RAIL ACCIDENTS All sorts of toxic liquids, solids, and gases are moved by railway. This is generally safer than transporting it by road, but the rails are not immune to accidents. Heat-warped tracks in the summer can send a row of cars off the rails, and operator errors can cause catastrophic collisions or derailments. Depending on the chemicals or materials that are spilled (and any reaction they may have together), and whether there is a fire, your best bet for action varies. Listen to the local news to make your decision whether to stay or go, and if you do decide to run, don't waste time packing and fussing over details. If you have a BOB (bug out bag) standing by, great. If not, grab your phone, wallet, and keys—and run.

AIRBORNE DANGER The instant you learn of a hazmat problem involving poison gas or other airborne toxins nearby, move indoors to limit exposure (unless you're told to evacuate). In especially bad cases, authorities may advise sealing your home. Here's how to do that safely.

First, shut any vents leading to the outside, including the fireplace damper. Turn off all air conditioners, fans, and ventilation systems.

Next, use plastic sheeting and duct tape to seal windows and doors. You can use aluminum foil or even wax paper to seal around air conditioner vents, kitchen and bathroom exhaust fans, and clothes dryer vents. Remember that even outlets and light switches let in fumes. Tape them up too.

Finally, close and lock exterior doors and windows so that no one can enter or leave after you seal the house. Once all that is done, move to an interior room to hunker down. Once you're inside with all needed supplies, seal off conduits into the room with duct tape, close all interior doors, and place towels at the bottom of doors to limit the air circulation within the house.

TROUBLE WITH THE WATER A mix-up at the water treatment facility is a rare event, but it could happen. In the event that the wrong chemicals or an excessive dose of the right chemicals (fluoride is pretty toxic stuff) enter the water supply, your recourse is easy—don't drink the water. But you

GOOD TO
KNOW

KNOW THE RISKS The modern international radiation scale measures exposure in gray units (Gy) rather than the older "rads." Here's how to understand a reading.

Gy	PHYSICAL CONDITION	CHANCE OF SURVIVAL
20+ / 11	SEIZURES AND TREMORS	MULTIPLE ORGAN FAILURE, DEATH CERTAIN
10 / 9 / 8	HYPOTENSION, SHOCK, VOMITING, ELECTROLYTE DISTURBANCE	DEATH CERTAIN WITHOUT STEM CELL TRANSPLANTS
7 / 6	DIARRHEA, HIGH FEVER, DISORIENTATION	DEATH LIKELY WITHIN WEEKS WITHOUT MEDICAL TREATMENT
5 / 4 / 3	BLEEDING, HAIR LOSS, INFECTIONS	DEATH POSSIBLE WITHIN MONTHS WITHOUT MEDICAL TREATMENT
2 / 1	NAUSEA, LOW BLOOD CELL COUNT, WEAKNESS	DEATH VERY UNLIKELY
0	SLIGHT DECREASE IN BLOOD CELL COUNT	NO RISK OF DEATH

have to know there's a problem to be able to boycott your kitchen faucet. One more reason to stay informed.

FIRE DOWN BELOW An accident down in the mines can lead to an underground coal fire, which can spew toxins aboveground. Although mine fires and explosions were much more common 100 years ago, even with more modern safety precautions they still pose a threat to the communities that live near mines today. If a mine does catch fire near you, seal up your home as you would for any other airborne contaminant, to keep the foul fumes and drifting smoke from entering your home.

GOOD TO
KNOW

HOW TO DECONTAMINATE YOURSELF

STEP ONE Strip off your clothes immediately after exposure to any toxins. This is no time for modesty, as even a couple of seconds can make a big difference. While you're undressing, avoid touching your eyes, mouth, or nose, as this could introduce more dangerous chemicals into your system.

STEP TWO Rinse every affected area for at least 15 minutes. If the hazardous material is also flammable, brush it off before stepping under the showerhead.

STEP THREE If your luck take a serious turn for the worse and you do end up with bad stuff in your eyes, rinse them out as well, rolling your eyes back and forth under the stream to cleanse as much of their surface area as possible.

TAKEN

A HOOD IS THROWN OVER YOUR HEAD AND YOU'RE DRAGGED INTO A VEHICLE. YOU TRY TO STRUGGLE FREE, BUT YOUR HANDS ARE BOUND AND YOU'RE POWERLESS. THERE ARE ONLY QUESTIONS NOW, NO ANSWERS. WHO ARE THESE MEN? WHAT DO THEY WANT? WHAT IF THEY DON'T GET IT?

Kidnapping and hostage situations are almost textbook examples of man's inhumanity toward man. While stranger abductions are rare occurrences, they do happen everywhere, and they're more common in rougher parts of the world. You are particularly at risk if you're engaged in shady business or if you look like a rich tourist. Most often, these circumstances occur over money, typically a lot of money. But kidnappings and hostage taking can happen for other reasons as well. Maybe someone doesn't want your family member to testify in court, or you were simply mistaken for someone else.

Whatever the reason is that you were taken captive, you can assume that you're dealing with people who are not afraid to break the law and hurt others. This is a precarious position you have fallen into, and it may be up to you to rescue yourself if the cavalry isn't coming. You'll need a variety of survival strategies at your fingertips, chiefly some escape and evasion techniques. And you'll need a lot of luck.

SPOT A TAIL, AND LOSE THEM

You've probably had that feeling that someone is following you. If you're on foot, slow down or stop and pretend to mess with your phone. Check to see if anyone slows down with you or walks past and then suddenly reappears later. To lose them, duck into a crowded coffee shop. Call some of your friends to come hang out. Leave as a group, because there's strength in numbers. If you think you're being tailed on the road, you need to know for certain. To do so, make four successive left turns. Someone might make one or two with you, but making all four is no coincidence. Lose the tail by making frequent lane changes, varying your speed, and traveling through well-populated areas. Drive to the police station if you're really alarmed.

THE STATS

8% Proportion of kidnapping victims, according to the FBI, who demonstrate signs of Stockholm syndrome.

20,000 Number of kidnappings that happen around the world each year, according to expert estimates.

1 IN 10 Number of those kidnappings that are reported to authorities.

220 YARDS (200 M) Distance from a victim's home or work in which most kidnappings occur.

50% Proportion of all global kidnappings that occur in Latin America.

70% Share of those kidnappings that result in the payment of a ransom.

10% Percentage of hostages who are rescued by force.

$2 MILLION Estimated amount, in USD, of the average ransom demand.

KIDNAPPING FOR RANSOM Kidnapping for ransom is nothing new. During the 1st century B.C.E., Roman nobility were sometimes kidnapped by Mediterranean pirates, and even a young Julius Caesar was once grabbed and held for ransom. After his release, he returned to them as he'd promised he would—but with a generous military force. He crucified each one of the kidnappers, at one hundred meter intervals along the Appian Way. Ransom kidnappings have changed little over the centuries, except that you're no longer allowed to rain down vengeance on your captors as Caesar did. Kidnappers still grab people. Some of their relatives call the authorities, and some don't. Most ransoms are paid by the family, and most captives are freed. But sadly, there are always exceptions. The hints below will help you cope in those situations and more.

OTHER KINDS OF ABDUCTIONS Occasionally, people are abducted and held hostage for reasons other than demanding a ransom in cash money. For example, a political candidate's family member might be snatched days before an election, causing him or her to drop out of the race. Key witnesses in criminal trials can be kidnap targets. Kidnap victims are also used or sold as slaves, forced to perform crimes, and even used as human shields.

Technically speaking, the most common form of kidnapping occurs when non-custodial parents take their children without the knowledge of the other parent. Even if the child wants to go with the parent, the criminal charge is still kidnapping.

That said, the scenario that parents find most scary is that of a child being grabbed by a stranger. While these cases are rare, those that do happen are heartbreaking and terrifying. Your first line of defense is to teach your kids about "stranger danger." Make sure they know that they should never go with a stranger, regardless of what the person says. They should never get into a vehicle, go into a room or building, or go to any new location with a stranger. They should never give out their address, name, or phone number to strangers. And finally, children should be taught to listen to their instincts. If any adult (even family

SKILL

ESCAPE FROM A CAR TRUNK Trapped in a trunk? You may just have to rescue yourself.

PULL THE TRUNK RELEASE If you're lucky, there will be a glow-in-the-dark T-handle trunk release. If not, look for the cable leading to the drivers' compartment trunk release and tug it toward the front of the car. This cable is usually along the floor on the driver's side.

USE SOME TOOLS Look for a screwdriver or tire iron you can use to pry the trunk latch open. Or use the tire jack to pry up a corner of the trunk lid, then signal other drivers for help.

KICK YOUR WAY OUT If the car's parked and empty, kick through the backseat and crawl out through the passenger compartment.

IF YOU'RE TRAPPED IN A CAR TRUNK AND ALL ELSE FAILS, TRY KICKING OUT ONE OF THE TAILLIGHTS. YOU MIGHT BE ABLE TO REACH AN ARM OUT AND WAVE FOR HELP.

friends and acquaintances) asks them to keep secrets, go with them unexpectedly, or do anything that makes them uncomfortable, the child should say "NO" loudly and go for help. Kids who are old enough and responsible enough to handle a smartphone should be taught to use one to call for help, or to snap photos of a threatening person or car. There have been cases in which would-be abductors have given up and run when a resourceful child texted pictures of their license plate to his parents.

SKILL

HUMANIZE YOURSELF. IF THE KIDNAPPERS SEE YOU AS A PERSON AS WELL AS A PAYDAY, YOU MAY RECEIVE BETTER TREATMENT FROM THEM. TALK ABOUT YOUR FAMILY AND HOW MUCH YOU LOVE AND MISS THEM.

PICK A ZIP TIE If you're not strong enough to break a zip tie (as we explained in Home Invasion, page 140), then maybe you can pick it like a lock.

Find something thin and hard to act as a shim. Insert it into the square part of the zip tie to lift up the metal locking blade that secures the tie opening. If this blade is lifted up, the tie should slide apart.

DEAL WITH A HOSTAGE SITUATION If you're taken hostage, don't just sit there and cry about it. There are things you can do to improve your odds of coming out alive—and helping the authorities foil the bad guys.

You can try to dial emergency services (if you can do so without being detected), and leave the line open so authorities can listen in. Some stores and banks even have an emergency button—if you can find it, push it.

If the situation goes on for any length of time, try to establish a rapport with your kidnappers. Yes, they're bad guys, but they probably have a human side (even Hitler liked animals). Try to get your captors to see your human side as well. You're better off if they view you as a person.

Always keep in mind that hostage-takers want to maintain a position of power and control. If you threaten

Two Months of Terror

On November 15, 1992, fishing guide Kjell von Sneidern and his friend were traveling the remote roads along the Orinoco River borderlands between Venezuela and Colombia. They were going to survey a remote location when they found that recently felled trees blocked the road. A group of twenty young men surrounded them and pulled the men from the vehicle at gunpoint. They took the two men into the jungle and demanded a $500,000 ransom.

For the next two months, the men were held captive. They traveled mostly at night to avoid detection. When resting, the captors would confine von Sneidern and his companion to hammocks, littering the ground beneath them with dry sticks and leaves to act as an alarm system. One of the captors carried a human skull with a bullet hole in it as a warning against trying to escape. Nature also worked to confound any attempt to escape. One spring they frequented was home to a 23-foot (7-m) anaconda,

and the jungle contained numerous jaguars. The two men endeavored to stay safe in captivity and gain the good will of their captors. They remained cooperative and gave their kidnappers their possessions as a means of winning them over. Local authorities were unsure how to respond, but von Sneidern's family sprang into action. They flew to the area, worked with officials, and hired mercenaries to follow the kidnappers and rescue the hostages. As they were tracked, the kidnappers became desperate, and many deserted. Those that remained commandeered a boat and made for the Venezuelan side of the river. But the boat's motor gave out and they drifted to shore, where Venezuelan authorities were waiting for them. Meanwhile, von Sneidern's family and hired guns stood guard on the Colombian side of the river.

When shooting broke out, von Sneidern and his friend jumped into the river. Finally, after 72 days of fear and suffering, a helicopter pulled the two men from the river.

A CARJACKING CAN EASILY TURN INTO A KIDNAPPING. AVOID BOTH SITUATIONS BY DRIVING WITH YOUR DOORS LOCKED AND LEAVING SOME ROOM TO MANEUVER AT STOP SIGNS AND LIGHTS.

that role, you put yourself at risk. So don't try to fight or run away (unless you feel very confident of your chances of escape). Sit where and how the hostage-takers tell you, and do exactly as they say. During interrogation, do not be uncooperative, antagonistic, or hostile towards your captors. Captives who display hostile behavior are often held longer or become the object of torture or punishment.

To stay ready for escape or rescue, you need to avoid falling into complacency. Every day, try to do some mental as well as physical exercise—you want to be feeling clear-headed and fit. If you can't move much, use isometric and flexing exercises to keep your muscles toned. Unless you think you're being drugged, eat what your captors give you—malnourishment makes you weak. And as for that very understandable stress, use meditation techniques to keep yourself from losing it.

Above all, pay attention. Your insight into the situation will be invaluable to law enforcement officials upon your release. Do your best to memorize detailed descriptions of the kidnappers (including how many there are). If you're

SKILL

ESCAPE FROM ROPES If your hands are tied, you can pull a Houdini-like escape with these tactics:

STEP ONE Begin by pushing and twisting the rope or cord to see if you can create a release of tension.

STEP TWO Grab the lines on both sides of the knot and push them together to loosen the knot.

STEP THREE Move your arms up and down to loosen the knot more. With persistence and luck, it will unravel.

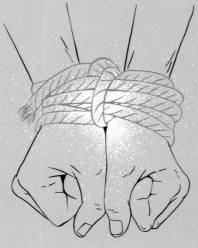

released before other hostages, take mental notes so you can describe where the remaining hostages are being kept.

IF A LOVED ONE IS KIDNAPPED The worst has happened: your loved one has been kidnapped. What can you do to help? The first and most important thing you can do is to contact the authorities. If this has happened in your home country, contact the local authorities or federal law enforcement. If the kidnapping has occurred abroad, try to reach your embassy or consulate to seek help. If you cannot reach either, then go to the local authorities or local government office. Whoever ends up assisting you, be patient with those who are helping you and do not expect a quick resolution to this personal crisis. Kidnappings are rarely resolved quickly.

~ T/F ~

STOCKHOLM SYNDROME IS A REAL THING

TRUE Stockholm syndrome is a form of traumatic bonding, named after the 1973 Norrmalmstorg robbery in Stockholm, Sweden. Several bank employees were held in a bank vault for six days. During the standoff, the hostages became attached to their kidnappers, and even defended them after being freed. Sometimes these positive feelings emerge simply because your kidnapper isn't abusing you, or because they are giving you food and drink. But remember, this is a criminal who is denying you freedom, and your survival is at risk. Pretend to cooperate, but don't forget the truth.

ACTS OF TERROR

TERRORISM SEEMS RANDOM TO THE VICTIMS, BUT THE SCARY FACT IS THAT SOMEONE HAD A PLAN. EVEN THOUGH THE MOTIVATIONS FOR AN ACT OF TERRORISM MAY BE UNCLEAR, THE DESIRED GOAL IS OBVIOUS. THEY WANTED TO SEE PEOPLE INJURED AND AFRAID, WHATEVER IT TAKES.

Throughout human history, there have been acts that threaten the security of nations. These actions have brought about loss of life, the destruction of property, illness and injury, the displacement of large numbers of people, and devastating economic loss. In contemporary times, technological advances and ongoing international political unrest give terrorists the tools and the motivation to become an even greater risk to global security.

The FBI makes the distinction between domestic and international terrorism, but the only real difference is who is doing the violence, and where it occurs. In both cases, terrorism is defined by violent acts that are intended to intimidate a civilian population and influence government. We traditionally think of terrorists as using explosives or nuclear, biological, or chemical agents. In the modern era, cyber terrorism is also an issue. Computer attacks can steal sensitive information, disable crucial government functions, or attack utilities such as the electrical grid or the water supply.

SPOT A CAR BOMB Car bombs are all too common in some parts of the world, but the unfortunate reality is that you could be at risk from one literally anywhere. Car bombers have been foiled when observant passersby noticed something off about a vehicle, so keep your eyes open. On the road, look for odd behavior from the driver. Watch for vehicles that are obviously carrying a heavy load, especially a heavy rear end on sedans and similar cars. Missing license plates can be a clue to something shady, as well as odd odors or smoke from a vehicle. If a car is parked for days in the same place, something might be up. If you see fuel jugs, exposed wiring, or wires going to a cell phone inside the vehicle, these are strong signs of a possible car bomb. Call 911 immediately.

THE STATS

9,700 Approximate number of worldwide terrorism incidents in 2013.

$3 TRILLION Total cost to the U.S. government for economic damage, security costs, and military and anti-terrorism funding as a result of the September 11, 2001 terrorist attacks.

90% Portion of terror attacks in the United States committed by non-Islamic organizations.

8 TIMES Amount more likely it is that you'll be killed by a lightning strike than a terror attack .

THE MATRIX

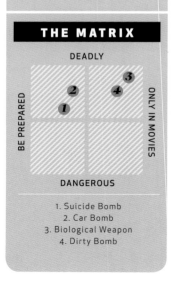

DEADLY

BE PREPARED

ONLY IN MOVIES

DANGEROUS

1. Suicide Bomb
2. Car Bomb
3. Biological Weapon
4. Dirty Bomb

TERRORISM We tend to think of terrorism as a modern phenomenon, but the concept and even the term have deep roots. While armed groups of zealots have battled those they saw as oppressors since biblical times, "terrorism" was first used to describe the violence committed by the government during the French Revolution. In the 1800s, explosives became more powerful and versatile, and increased globalization and communication made it easier for radical groups to have an effect.

Many historians consider the first modern terror attacks to be the bombings carried out in the 1880s by Irish nationalists protesting British occupation, and the first Middle Eastern incidents occurred as early as the 1920s. And while we think of terrorists as part of a larger group, some individual "lone wolf" madmen have changed history in terrible ways, such as Leon Czolgosz, the anarchist who assassinated President William McKinley for somewhat murky political reasons. Still, there's no question that modern weapons, communications technology, and the ease of global travel have created a whole new kind of terrorist threat.

As throughout history, these acts can be committed by a deranged lone wolf, or by a well-organized and well-funded group. Despite their differences, their goals are usually the same—to create terror, chaos, and disruption, and to cause loss of life. Here are some ways you can hope to foil or fight back against these hate-filled attacks. Or, in a worst-case scenario, at least survive.

SPOT A SUICIDE BOMBER Suicide bombing has been around since the early 1980s, at the very least. Attacks of this kind have happened in Israel, Lebanon, and more recently, in Iraq. This has become such a common occurrence in some places that the military and law enforcement have had to adapt their tactics to take this weapon into account. A suicide bomber usually carries 11–29 pounds (5–13 kg) of explosives, inside a vest or a bag. These explosives are commonly packed with nails, ball bearings, and other metal pieces that act as shrapnel and maximize the injuries and fatalities from the bombing.

Bombers aren't always easy to spot. Someone wearing a bulky or long coat to cover an explosive vest might stand out in hot weather. But a person carrying a bag, box, backpack, or suitcase will probably go unnoticed. Nevertheless, you can still look for sketchy behavior in crowded places. And be aware that double bombings have been used to kill first responders who are trying to help the victims of the first bomb. If a bombing occurs near you, try to reach cover in case a second one goes off.

CAR BOMBINGS Car bombs are a much bigger and more devastating version of hand-carried bombs or the suicide bomb. A vehicle may be laden with gunpowder, dynamite, TNT, nitroglycerin, ammonium nitrate fertilizer, or fuel. More organized groups may even have access to C4, PETN, or Semtex explosives. Look for any of the markers already mentioned in this section, to avoid a potential car bomb. These signs can make a difference. The 2010 Times Square car bombing attempt was foiled when two street vendors spotted smoke coming from a vehicle. They alerted an NYPD patrolman, who called in the bomb squad.

> IF YOU SEE SOMETHING THAT DOESN'T LOOK RIGHT, SMELL RIGHT, OR SOUND RIGHT, OR A PERSON ACTING STRANGELY, CALL THE AUTHORITIES. IN SHORT, IF YOU SEE SOMETHING, SAY SOMETHING.

TERRORIST CAUSES CAN SEEM ROMANTIC TO YOUNG PEOPLE. IF ANYONE YOU KNOW TALKS ABOUT RUNNING OFF TO JOIN THE "FREEDOM FIGHTERS" ABROAD, TAKE THEM SERIOUSLY. YOU MIGHT SAVE A LIFE.

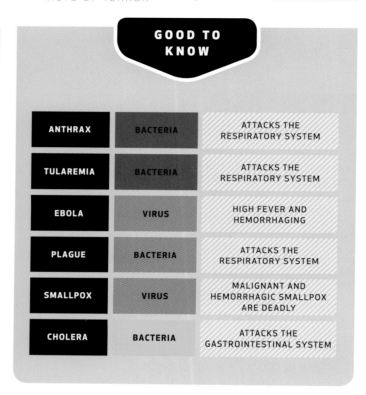

GOOD TO KNOW

ANTHRAX	BACTERIA	ATTACKS THE RESPIRATORY SYSTEM
TULAREMIA	BACTERIA	ATTACKS THE RESPIRATORY SYSTEM
EBOLA	VIRUS	HIGH FEVER AND HEMORRHAGING
PLAGUE	BACTERIA	ATTACKS THE RESPIRATORY SYSTEM
SMALLPOX	VIRUS	MALIGNANT AND HEMORRHAGIC SMALLPOX ARE DEADLY
CHOLERA	BACTERIA	ATTACKS THE GASTROINTESTINAL SYSTEM

BIOLOGICAL WEAPONS Pathogenic organisms can be used to kill or incapacitate people, destroy food crops, or kill livestock. These nasty bugs can also be used to contaminate air, water, and soil. Terrorists and rogue nations favor the ones that are highly toxic, easy to obtain, and/or inexpensive to produce. Also high on the bad guys' wish list are weaponized pathogens that are easily passed from person to person and/or can be incorporated into materials that are easy to disperse. And, of course, those diseases with no known vaccine or good treatment are especially sought after. Above, just a few of the pathogens and materials that keep the bio-security folks up at night.

DEAL WITH A DIRTY BOMB Any explosive device with a radioactive component would be considered a "dirty bomb." These would cause far greater fear in a population than just an explosion of the same magnitude. A dirty

GOOD TO KNOW

DEATH ON WHEELS Sometimes the vehicle used for a bomb is a matter or availability, but sometimes the goal is mass destruction. Here's a guide to knowing how far to run, if you're lucky enough to be warned in time.

TYPE OF VEHICLE	MAXIMUM EXPLOSIVES CAPACITY	LETHAL AIR BLAST RANGE	MINIMUM EVACUATION DISTANCE
	500 LBS 227 KG	100 FT 30 M	1,500 FT 457 M
	1,000 LBS 455 KG	125 FT 38 M	1,750 FT 534 M
	4,000 LBS 1,818 KG	200 FT 61 M	2,750 FT 838 M
	10,000 LBS 4,545 KG	300 FT 91 M	3,750 FT 1,143 M
	30,000 LBS 13,636 KG	450 FT 137 M	6,500 FT 1,982 M
	60,000 LBS 27,273 KG	600 FT 183 M	7,000 FT 2,134 M

bomb spreads radioactive particles throughout the blast radius, which then drift downwind and are also tracked by people and vehicles throughout the area. The fear caused by a bombing is one thing, but the fear of getting cancer or having other health issues in the future puts this weapon on a whole different level. If a dirty bomb is suspected or confirmed in your area, shelter in place and seal off your home as you would for an industrial accident (see page 157).

(see page 157)

T/F

TERRORISTS ARE BASICALLY COMMON CRIMINALS

FALSE While terrorists commit terrible crimes, they cannot be viewed the same way as other criminals. Criminals tend to be poor and uneducated; many terrorists by contrast actually come from relatively well-off families, and are often well-educated. This matters, because it means they are likely to have the resources to plan complex attacks, and the money to more easily evade capture. Osama Bin Laden, arguably the worst terrorist of our time, was the son of a billionaire and had a massive network of supporters and hideouts.

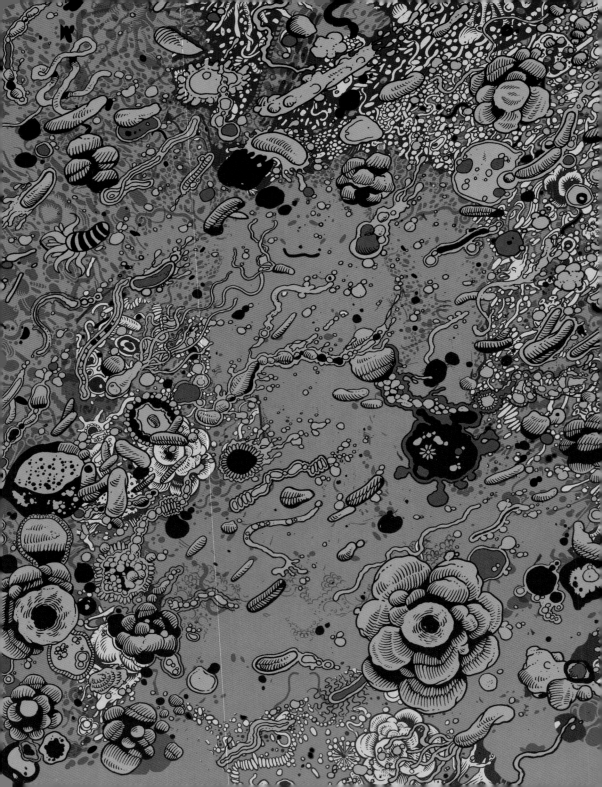

CONTAGIONS

ALTHOUGH THE "BLACK DEATH" IS LARGELY CONFINED TO HISTORY BOOKS, THE THREAT OF A WORLDWIDE EPIDEMIC IS AN EVER-PRESENT ONE. HISTORICAL DISEASES COULD RE-EMERGE AND NEW PATHOGENS ARE BEING TOYED WITH EVERY DAY. SOME DOCTORS SAY "IT'S NOT IF, BUT WHEN…"

There is comfort in knowing that modern medicine can conquer the diseases that laid our ancestors low through recorded history. Except for a few present-day cases, anthrax, yellow fever, and the bubonic plague seem to have almost vanished from the world. Once a death sentence, these maladies can now be treated and cured with basic medicines that any doctor can prescribe, at least when they occur in the developed world. But are we lulled into a false sense of security, when wonder drugs are commonly available in any pharmacy?

Some of the world's diseases are still very hard to treat, and fatal if they have advanced too far before treatment begins. Sometimes diseases evolve to become more deadly. In addition, intentionally "weaponized" or modified diseases could be unleashed on an unsuspecting planet, through accident or terrorist attack. The world's not as safe as it seems to be, when the next pandemic lurks in a bio-weapons lab or in an international traveler's cough.

WHAT IS A PANDEMIC? You may be wondering what the difference is between an outbreak and an epidemic, as they're quite similar. Both are defined as a widespread occurrence of an infectious disease within a community; the difference between the two is the disease's death rate. There are no hard and fast numerical rules to differentiate the two, and many factors are considered. But generally, an epidemic is an outbreak of any disease that has higher mortality rates than normal for that disease. If an epidemic occurs across several countries and affects a large percentage of the population in each, it is considered a pandemic. Recent pandemics include the Hong Kong flu in 1968 and 1969, and we can all recall the 2009 H1N1 pandemic.

THE STATS

33,000 Average yearly number of deaths from influenza and related illnesses in the U.S.

95% Odds of becoming infected with measles by being in the same room as a carrier of the disease.

75 MILLION Estimated number of worldwide deaths from the Black Plague in the 14th century. (Repeated outbreaks occurred in Europe, Asia, and North America well into the 20th century; minor incidents continue across the globe today.)

65% Average fatality rate of victims infected with Ebola virus. (Rates can run as high as 95% without proper treatment.)

99% Percentage of germs eliminated by proper use of hand sanitizer.

36,000 Deaths from the flu in the U.S. in an average year.

37 Number of countries where SARS spread within a few weeks in 2003.

BACTERIA VS VIRUSES All kinds of organisms can be harmful to human life, but the two most common troublemakers are bacteria and viruses. Both can kill, and they're often confused with each other, but they're actually very different forms of life. Bacteria are the oldest creatures on Earth, and can be found in a wide range of shapes and sizes, some helpful to human life and some lethal. Viruses are small infectious agents that enter living cells (in animals, plants, and even bacteria) and replicate themselves. The vast majority of viruses and bacteria can be rendered harmless by our immune system.

CONTAINED BY MODERN MEDICINE Mercifully, some of our worst biological foes have been successfully removed from the world's population. Smallpox was once common; it killed between 300 million and 500 million people in the 20th century alone. After decades of vaccination campaigns, the last case in the U.S. happened in 1949, and the last case globally occurred in Somalia in 1977. The World Health Organization declared smallpox eradicated in 1979, and now the disease only exists in a few vials scattered through the world. Why keep any of it? In the event that the disease resurfaces, as a terrorist's bio-weapon or by some natural cause, original samples could be invaluable in creating new vaccines and treatments.

COMMON DISEASES, DEADLY VARIANTS Near the end of World War I, the Spanish influenza of 1918 killed somewhere between 40 million and 100 million people worldwide. This especially deadly form of the H1N1 influenza virus began killing people in January 1918, and continued until December 1920. This flu was unusual in its high mortality rate, and its tendency to kill relatively healthy people. In most influenza outbreaks, those with weakened immune systems are at the greatest risk of death. In the Spanish influenza, healthy young adults were the primary fatalities, while the young, the elderly, and those with weakened immune systems survived the illness. It's believed that this influenza infected more than 500 million people across the globe (even in the Arctic and remote

SKILL

WASH LIKE A SURGEON Nothing fights germs like frequent and thorough hand washing. Even though we've been washing our hands without help since childhood, it's smart to consider the hand-washing details that doctors employ. Short fingernails, good washing technique, warm water, and ample soap might just stop the next pandemic before it starts.

STEP 1 Turn on the warm water and wet your hands.

STEP 2 Apply soap to the palms, and backs of your hands.

STEP 3 Rub your soapy palms together.

STEP 4 Rub your palm on the back of your hand, threading the fingers of your top hand between your lower fingers.

STEP 5 Rub your palms together, interlacing your fingers and scrubbing them.

STEP 6 Bend your fingers under, face your hands palm to palm, and scrub your fingernails together.

STEP 7 Wash each thumb by using the opposite hand to twist it.

STEP 8 Using your fingernails, scrub the palm of each hand in a circular motion.

STEP 9 Rinse both hands with warm water.

STEP 10 Dry your hands with a disposable paper towel.

STEP 11 Turn off the water, using the paper towel as a barrier to the faucet handle.

A LIGHT COATING OF VASELINE OR NEOSPORIN IN YOUR NOSTRILS CAN PROTECT AGAINST AIRBORNE GERMS ON PLANES AND TRAINS AND IN CROWDED SPACES. BLOW YOUR NOSE TO REMOVE THE OILY FILM LATER.

T/F

USING TOO MUCH HAND SANITIZER MIGHT LEAD TO "SUPERBUGS"

TRUE It's a proven fact that improper use of antibiotics can create health problems. A recent study of 161 long-term care facilities found that when hand sanitizer is used instead of soap and water, there is a link to outbreaks of highly infectious norovirus. Fifty-three percent of the facilities that reported a preference for hand sanitizer had confirmed norovirus outbreaks, in contrast to 18 percent of facilities with soap and water preference. Clean hands save lives, but how you clean them may be equally important.

Pacific islands). Of the infected, 50 to 100 million of them died from the illness, roughly 3–5 percent of the world's population at the time.

NEW BUGS EMERGE As germs mutate and spread through speedy global travel and commerce, it shouldn't surprise anyone that new bugs are emerging to harass the world's populace. One of the newest is MERS, the Middle East Respiratory Syndrome, first described in 2012. MERS is a virus that causes coughing, fever, and sometimes a fatal pneumonia-like complication that accounts for its high fatality rate. MERS is a coronavirus from the same family as SARS, or Severe Acute Respiratory Syndrome.

If you remember the SARS scare, that virus killed about 800 people worldwide after first appearing in China in 2002, and had a 9-12 percent mortality rate, which means that the vast majority of people who contracted it survived. By comparison, there have been 572 cases of MERS in 15 countries over two years, with a 30 percent death rate.

MRSA (Methicillin-resistant Staphylococcus aureus) is another relatively new threat, caused by an antibiotic-resistant strain of staph bacteria. It poses a risk to health-care workers, those who have been treated at medical facilities, and the general public.

A SLOW BUT DEADLY INCREASE One of the most recent widespread panics we've faced surrounds the incredibly deadly and contagious Ebola virus. While fears of it spreading rapidly through the developed world seem to have proven to be overblown (for now), and with the right tools it is indeed treatable, the fact is that this horrific disease is devastating areas of Africa and, as we learned from the HIV crisis, viruses can spread unexpectedly quickly and in unpredicted ways.

The first case of Ebola was reported in 1976, and there were no other outbreaks for almost 20 years, until 2014 in West Africa. In general, the Ebola virus's death rate ranges from 25–90 percent and averages at around 50 percent—overall a shocking toll, especially if the virus mutates to become less treatable.

GOOD TO KNOW

LAB ACCIDENTS HAPPEN In April of 1979, anthrax spores were accidentally released at a military research compound in the town of Sverdlovsk, Russia. This incident later became known as the "biological Chernobyl." The anthrax outbreak reportedly caused over 100 deaths, though the exact details may never be known. The medical records surrounding this outbreak were seized by the Russian government, as this incident was in serious violation of the Biological Weapons Convention. Anthrax exposure can result in death within two days to a month. Most deaths occur about eight days after exposure, and alarmingly, antibiotic-resistant strains of anthrax are known. Could this happen again? Or something worse? Experts say yes, and labs are full of even more deadly diseases.

CREATE A CLEAN ROOM In the event of a major epidemic, you may not have access to a modern medical facility, but you'll still need a way to quarantine sick people. Setting up an army tent in the back yard would be the safest way to separate the ill people from the healthy ones, but it's not an affordable or applicable option for most households. By contrast, an isolation room can be set up almost anywhere, cheaply and quickly. With some caution and few supplies, you can set up a "sick room" in your home to care for ill family and friends, while reducing the chance of spreading the disease throughout your group.

Ideally, you'd have a guest room with its own bathroom, windows for ventilation, away from the main traffic areas of the home. Realistically, since most of us don't have that kind of space, you may have to settle for an out-of-the-way bedroom with a bucket for a toilet.

If the electrical grid stays up during this bio-disaster, and the home has central air conditioning and/or heating, you'll need to block off the air flow to the isolation room. Cover

DON'T FORGET ABOUT EYE PROTECTION WHEN YOU'RE SHOPPING FOR MASKS. ALL OF THE BREATHING PROTECTION ON EARTH WON'T HELP YOU IF AN INFECTED PERSON SNEEZES INTO YOUR EYES.

floor and wall vents tightly with duct tape. Never choose a room for an isolation room if it has an air return for the AC or heating system. This could suck in bacteria and viruses, and spread them throughout the home.

Once this room is set up, only one person should be acting as the caregiver to the infected person (or persons). They should wear coveralls, a mask, gloves, and goggles. They should have a pair of slip-on shoes, that are only to be worn in the isolation room, and that remain outside the door when not in use. An apron or smock can be made from a large trash bag by cutting arm and head holes in one end. This could go over the coveralls as extra protection from bodily fluids, or to protect your clothing if you don't have coveralls.

When exiting the room, spray down your protective gear with disinfectant and wait one minute before disrobing from contaminated protective gear.

Outside of the isolation room door, place a trash can with a lid. This will be the receptacle for anything contaminated by contact with the infected person or the room. Disinfecting spray should also be stationed outside the door. It should be used on the trash can, the door knob, and any potentially contaminated surfaces in the isolation room and outside of it.

Nothing inside the room should come out, if at all possible. Dishes, cups and utensils for the infected should be disposable, and discarded in a trash bag inside the isolation room. Sheets and bedding should be washed in hot water with bleach, and hung to dry in the room if possible. A sheet of plastic between the mattress and bedding will keep the mattress from absorbing blood, vomit and other bodily fluids.

The isolation room should be cleaned daily, with all solid surfaces wiped down by a disinfectant. Have your patient wear a standard surgical mask to minimize the dangerous droplets they expel from coughing and sneezing.

Finally, your patient should have an easy way to signal for help, as they may be too weak to call out. A bell, rattle, or some similar noise making gizmo should be with your patient's reach.

PANDEMIC SUPPLIES When disease strikes, you'll need the right supplies to help protect the healthy from the sick. Here's a list of items that would be very useful, should that horseman ride through your town.

TYVEK COVERALLS These are tough, tear-proof, and almost waterproof. They're available at most hardware stores, and can be purchased with head and shoe covers.

MASKS A variety of standard medical masks, N95 masks, or even a few N100s could be invaluable. Buy a giant box of them at a warehouse store, and you'll have plenty leftover for trade goods.

GOGGLES AND GLOVES Lab goggles or work goggles are the best choices, especially with an anti-fog coating and vents. A case of nitrile gloves will protect your hands, without causing latex allergies.

PLASTIC SHEETING AND DUCT TAPE These can seal off doors, windows, vents, and more. They're also handy for covering mattresses and dead bodies.

LARGE TRASH BAGS Use them for trash, wear them as aprons, or use them as barriers—hundreds of uses.

LYSOL OR SIMILAR DISINFECTING SPRAY A case of these disinfecting spray cans could save your family.

HAND SANITIZER Everyone should be using this—very often—during any infectious event.

CHLORINE BLEACH Bleach can be a great disinfectant for laundry and makes sanitizing solution.

THERMOMETER Get several inexpensive thermometers. Check each patient's temperature with their own unit. Don't share. Disposable forehead thermometers are an option, though not as easy to read.

OLD FOES CAN RESURFACE Numerous previously unknown organisms have been found in recent years in liquefying permafrost and glacial ice. It can't be ruled out that these organisms may be harmful to modern humans, or our livestock and plants. If organisms were deadly to humans in the remote past, any immunity that we once carried may be long gone. One gruesome possibility is that long-frozen infected corpses could resurface, thaw, and spread smallpox anew.

For example, in 2014, a 30,000-year-old virus was found in melting Siberian permafrost, and was determined to still be contagious (although, luckily, not to humans). However, it's entirely likely that long-lost pathogens from our remote ancestors are out there, frozen, waiting to be revived and wreak havoc once again.

ARMED MADMAN

LOUD BANGS RING OUT IN THE OFFICE. WERE THOSE GUNSHOTS? ONE MINUTE YOU'RE SITTING AT YOUR DESK WONDERING WHAT TO HAVE FOR LUNCH, THE NEXT YOU'RE RUNNING FOR YOUR LIFE. HERE'S HOW TO SURVIVE WHEN AN ARMED LUNATIC STARTS A SHOOTING SPREE.

Senseless violence in crowded places is nothing new in the world—indeed, the term "berserker" dates back to over a thousand years ago, when it was used to describe the insane fighting of Norse warriors. Still, modern life has brought a new kind of terror to these violent encounters. Everyday people go about their lives aware that at any moment, unexpected and deadly violence could erupt in any public space anywhere in the country.

Whether you are trapped in a building, assaulted in your workplace, or targeted in a shopping mall or theater, you're a sitting duck when someone armed and dangerous decides to open fire. Your first instinct may be to cower or run, but you won't be alone. The shooter may be expecting people to crowd at the exit, and this could be a tempting target. So what do you do if heading for the exit seems too dangerous? Staying alert is critically important, but there are also a variety of tactics that you could use to boost your chances of survival in this tragic circumstance.

DEFUSE THE SITUATION Should you ever try to defuse a violent situation in the workplace? It's a challenging question that could ultimately mean life or death for yourself and your coworkers. If a coworker brings a weapon into the building and begins to talk about using it, your intervention could save lives and get your troubled team member the help he needs. But this bravery could also make you victim number one. If the person has already started shooting, it's too late to engage him in friendly dialogue. But if it's a coworker you have a rapport with and things haven't turned violent yet, you could try to talk him out of it. Stay wary, and if it looks as though he's ignoring your words, or getting irrationally angry, don't hesitate to make an excuse and exit quickly.

12 Average number of mass shootings (legally defined as an event involving 3 or more victims) per year in the United States.

78% Percentage of workplace homicides involving guns.

49% Percentage of shootings involving a semiautomatic handgun.

4 TO 1 Ratio of male to female workplace homicide victims.

100 Times more likely that a child is to die outside of school than at school.

39% Percentage of U.S. households that have at least one gun.

44 Number of people killed in America's deadliest school attack, the Bath School disaster in 1927. (58 more were injured.)

14 Number of people killed by a disgruntled Oklahoma postal worker in 1986, inspiring the phrase "going postal."

RUN, HIDE, FIGHT In an unexpected attack, one natural human instinct is to crouch and stay still. But freezing is the last thing you should do. A better course of action is one that's taught in law enforcement circles: the principle of run, hide, fight. This simple set of instructions teaches you first to run from the attacker. You are also encouraged to bring people with you, those who may be frozen with fear or uncertain what to do. If there's no clear exit to run from the situation, the next action is to hide. Hiding should take place in a spot that offers protection, ideally a place where you cannot be shot. If both of those options aren't available, then fighting is your last resort to survive.

TRY EVASIVE MANEUVERS As you run or move in an active shooter situation, you'll want to make yourself a hard target to hit. If you've ever spent time shooting, you know it can be hard enough to hit a stationary target when you're not sure of the range (distance to the target). If you add in erratic movement and obstacles, the target (in this case, you) becomes much harder to hit.

Your first imperative is to keep moving— a moving target is much harder to hit. Move in an unpredictable zigzag pattern to prevent the shooter from aiming at a spot where you're "going to be," and head toward cover or an exit. Crouch low as you move and, if you have to climb over an obstacle, keep a low profile.

If at all possible, get out. Any exit is better than no exit, unless the shooter is killing people crowded at that exit. Find a way out, perhaps an unexpected or unorthodox egress, to minimize your chance of getting caught. Jump out a low window, shimmy down a fire escape, or use a rooftop exit.

If there's not an exit you can bolt to easily, your next goal is to get to cover. Take shelter behind solid objects that can provide a shield between you and the shooter. Silence your cell phone if you're hiding: one ring can give you away.

DISARM A SHOOTER Let me approach this topic with the proviso that this is almost certainly a very bad idea. But there have been shooting cases where potential victims

GOOD TO KNOW

If you're in danger from a sniper, whether a professional gone rogue or a madman perched on a clock tower, you need to do everything possible to reduce his accuracy.

STICK TO THE SHADOWS Like any shooter, snipers prefer a well-lit target. Someone shooting randomly will be less likely to target you if you stay in darker, shadowed areas, and move stealthily to avoid drawing his eye.

BE UNPREDICTABLE The sniper will be "leading the target," planning his shot based on your position and pace. Changing speed and direction can throw him off.

AVOID LANDMARKS If the shooter lacks laser sighting, he can target using known objects as a reference. If you're standing near a street sign, that's a tip-off as to your size and distance, making you easier to hit.

were able to disarm the shooter when he stopped to reload. Keep in mind that an experienced shooter can reload in seconds, so this window won't last long. You'd have to be ready to pounce the second that the shooter realizes he's out of ammunition. Control the weapon and attack the shooter as ferociously as you can. If possible, convince others to attack as a group.

SHOULD YOU PLAY DEAD? If you can't escape, can't disarm the shooter, or there are multiple shooters, your only way to live may be to play dead. Lie facedown on the floor and let your belly expand with each inward breath, not your ribs. Your position will conceal the movement of your belly and it will appear that you're not breathing. If you can go completely limp and relax every muscle in your body (which is tough in a tense situation), this will allow your body to move correctly if you are prodded by a shooter. To anyone viewing you, you'll appear freshly deceased.

T / F

IT'S ALWAYS THE QUIET ONES WHO BECOME VIOLENT

FALSE The sullen loner types aren't the only people who could snap. Men and women of diverse ages have been workplace shooters. Some of the most serious signs to watch for are a new fascination with weapons (particularly guns), an obsession with police tactics, threats toward coworkers or other people, a new religious fervor or political affiliation, violent entertainment, a decline in hygiene and relationship skills, and significant changes in behavior. Speak to someone in HR if a coworker begins to fit the profile.

TROUBLE ABROAD

ROBBED AND PENNILESS IN A FOREIGN LAND, WITH NO FRIENDS OR ANYONE TO TURN TOWARD FOR HELP. YOU DON'T UNDERSTAND THE LANGUAGE OR THE LAWS. BUT APPARENTLY YOU BROKE THE RULES. SEVERAL MEN IN UNIFORMS ARE MOVING TOWARD YOU OMINOUSLY.

Travel can be one of life's great joys, but it can also open you up to a whole new world of potential troubles. There's a reason the term "getting out of your comfort zone" is a double-edged sword. You should never let fear of the unknown constrain you, but neither should you be foolhardy. Some situations that commonly arise overseas can be anticipated and planned for, such as taking precautions in case you are robbed. Other situations are much more rare, but also much scarier, such as being caught up in a civil war or the fall of a government.

Your best defense is to get educated about your destination before you leave. Take the time to learn about the people and their culture. Find out about the most common threats to travelers in that place, and keep an eye on current events. It is crucial that you make note of your country's embassy or consulate. This can be a source of assistance in case you have any problems during your travels, or even a refuge if something goes horribly wrong.

DON'T STICK OUT The last thing you want to look like when traveling is a tourist, especially a rich tourist. Don't call attention to yourself. Try to look like a local by buying some appropriate local clothing and footwear when you arrive. If everyone wears a beard in that land, then stop shaving a few months before the trip. If you're a woman, you may find that standards of dress are much more modest than at home, even in European countries. Some countries have very particular local standards of dress, and you ignore them at your peril. Even if you don't become a target of kidnapping or major theft, you don't want to draw the ire of local enforcers by wearing a tank top or open-toed shoes that seem completely innocent to you, but are seen as an insult to local ways.

THE STATS

$500 MILLION Estimated yearly amount collected by criminal gangs in kidnap and ransom payments.

11 Number of American citizens known to be currently held captive or missing abroad.

8 YEARS Longest time (so far) an American has been held captive by a foreign party; Robert Levinson has been detained by Iranian authorities since 2007.

58 Number of nations that still carry out the death penalty (in some cases, for crimes involving drug possession).

2,500 Number of U.S. citizens who are arrested overseas each year.

30% Estimated proportion of those arrests that are drug related.

6 Number of cane strokes an American teenager was sentenced to receive in 1994 in Singapore, for vandalism. (It was reduced to four when President Clinton intervened.)

TRAVEL WITHOUT TROUBLE There are plenty of things you can do to prepare for travel to scarier locales, and helpful things you can do while you're there. Here are some of the top methods to stay out of trouble. In fact, most of these tips are a good idea even if you're just taking a road trip to the Grand Canyon with the family. But they become even more crucial the farther from home you are.

First, always bring your driver's license. Many nations honor driver's licenses from other countries, and your license may allow you to rent a car. You never know when that might come in handy in a pinch. In addition, it's also a great piece of secondary ID. Your primary ID on the road is, of course, your passport. Keep it hidden somewhere on your person, because if you lose that you might not get out of that country at all. Even in what you think is a safe place, don't let the passport out of your sight.

Always have at least one credit card with a high spending limit to buy last-minute plane tickets, which are incredibly expensive. On a day-to-day basis, keep local currency on you, for bribes, food, transportation, whatever.

Have a check-in plan set up before your trip, or set a plan up at the first sign of unexpected trouble when you are already overseas. Have a friend, family member, or coworker expecting a phone call from you at a certain time every day. If the call doesn't come through, he should go to the authorities within an agreed amount of time.

Be familiar with the local transportation. What do the local taxi cabs look like? How do you spot a fake taxi that would drive you down a back alley and rob you? How do you catch the bus? What does an official bus look like? (There have been horrifying stories of criminals driving a around in a bus to pick up and assault unsuspecting riders.) What parasites would you catch if you rode a pack animal? There are many things to consider when learning the local transportation system. Learn them. It matters.

LEAVE IT AT HOME Leave copies of all of your documents with a trusted person back home. This should include passports, credit card information, driver's license, birth certificate, medical insurance papers, and any other

CAN'T DO WITHOUT

WATER PURIFIER No one needs to get sick while traveling, and rougher parts of the world are notorious for contaminated drinking water. One of the most convenient devices for water disinfection is the portable UV purifier. It dishes out a lethal dose of ultraviolet light, killing or disabling waterborne pathogens. These pocket-sized UV purifiers typically run on two AA batteries and work with push-button ease. Stick the light bulb element into a glass of water, hit the button, and stir the bulb during the 45 second cycle of glowing blue light. For maximum effect, you can zap the water twice.

important documents you feel they should have. Other things you won't want to bring with you during travel are expensive electronics, jewelry, and any other items that make you a target for robbery—or worse, a candidate for kidnapping. If you can live without them, leave them behind. One exception though, is bringing a mobile phone that works at your destination. This could be a lifesaver. Guard it carefully—phone theft is common around the world. Don't walk and text or check Facebook on the train.

DON'T DRINK THE WATER Be aware of things that can make you sick—drinking the water, but also eating food that's been washed in dirty water. Also, that bottled water might

T / F

BRING YOUR OWN MEDICAL SUPPLIES ABROAD

FALSE Fear of shoddy health standards in poverty-stricken nations has led some to travel with their own syringes and emergency meds. The thing is, this might just make you look like a drug user to the suspicious authorities. Unless you have a specific medical condition (like diabetes, in which you'd need medicines and needles) or you are a doctor traveling to somewhere where there's a current outbreak of something, leave the medical gear at home. The odds you'll need an injection are low, and you can always demand that needles be sterilized.

DIPLOMATIC RELATIONS
At the time of writing, the U.S. had a diplomatic presence in virtually every nation with very few exceptions, including the expected (North Korea) and some less-expected cases (Guinea-Bissau, Bhutan). Often, the embassy in a nearby nation handles issues (for Bhutan, it's India), but this may not be much help if communications go down. If you're a U.S. citizen or any other English-speaking citizen of the world, the U.S. State Department website is loaded with sound travel advice, and more importantly - travel advisories and warnings about dangerous areas. Criminal activity against travelers, terrorist activity, military conflicts, and many other hazards are explained and updated on their website, at travel.state.gov.

not be so clean either. Don't be paranoid, but don't be stupid about your health, either. Add the phrase "I want a beer, in the bottle, and I'll uncap it myself, thank you" to your phrasebook before you go. Be in charge of your food, water, and medicines as much as possible. If turmoil or mayhem erupts while you're there, don't expect the supply chain to be unaffected. Have some back-ups in place, like a stash of food and drinks where you are staying. Select stuff that would be tamper evident, as a way for your stuff to guard itself while you are gone. Protein bars and sealed packages of dried fruit and/or nuts are good.

SURVIVE IN LOCK-UP What to do if you're thrown in prison unfairly, framed for a crime you didn't commit, or just for the crime of being a foreigner? Also, remember that many countries have much harsher laws than the U.S. Thailand, India, Iran, and many other countries are exceedingly tough on drug crimes, particularly foreigners moving drugs in or out of the country, a stupid mistake more than one college student has made. If you do end up in lock-up, put up no fight with the authorities, other than to make sure that your family knows where you are. For American travelers, the State Department's Office of American Citizen Services and Crisis Management (ACS) supports the overseas embassies and consulates in providing emergency services to Americans, including legal help.

Nightmare Overseas

British scientist William Sampson was working in Saudi Arabia as a consultant when his horrifying story began. In December 2000, he was arrested after a rash of car bombings left one British engineer dead and several others severely wounded. The Saudis believed that the bombings were perpetrated by other Westerners. Sampson had been in Saudi Arabia for over two years and was familiar enough with the land and its laws to know that he was in dire trouble, though he didn't know just how bad his nightmare would be.

In a detainment facility, Sampson was chained up in a standing position to his cell door, which prevented him from sleeping and led to terrorizing hallucinations. Sampson was also periodically hung upside down while interrogators beat the soles of his feet, his legs, back, and groin. He was hog-tied, whipped, and kicked.

Sampson's accusers repeatedly tortured him, then lectured him on his crimes, and finally tried to convince him to confess. While he maintained that he was innocent, his captors continued their merciless torture. After six days of constant pain, no sleep, and unbelievable torture, Sampson's will was broken.

He wrote an admission of guilt that he planted and detonated the bomb that killed his British colleague. He hoped that with this confession, albeit false, his torture would end. Though he was certain he would be sentenced to death by beheading, Sampson had slid to a point beyond the fear of death. Yet his torture and captivity continued.

For two years, seven months, three weeks, and two days, the innocent Sampson was held against his will and tortured. He was finally freed along with eight other Westerners who were held in connection with the 2000 bombings. This was only after Saudi King Fahd agreed to release the Westerners in exchange for terror suspects held by the U.S. at Guantánamo Bay.

PIRATES AHOY!

GONE ARE THE PIRATES OF OLD, SWASHBUCKLING THEIR WAY ACROSS THE HIGH SEAS. IN THEIR WAKE, THE MODERN PIRATE EMERGES. WITH AUTOMATIC WEAPONS AND THE LATEST TECHNOLOGY, THEY HAUNT TROUBLED WATERS AND PREY ON LONE SHIPS, CONTINUING THE BLOODY TRADITION.

Piracy has existed for thousands of years. The earliest accounts are from the 14th century B.C.E., when seafaring peoples threatened merchant ships in the Aegean and Mediterranean. Today's pirates complete the same vicious work as their forebears, namely acts of robbery and murder on ships. But these aren't the only violations of maritime law that pirates perform. Extortion, hostage-taking, kidnapping for ransom, seizure of the ship, and wholesale destruction are also common practices of the contemporary pirate.

Since the end of the Cold War, the navies of many countries have been downsized, and global trade has increased. These factors (more ships and fewer authorities) have allowed a resurgence of piracy in recent years. Some modern brigands are tied to organized-crime syndicates, heavily armed and experienced, while others are small and amateurish groups, poorly armed and disorganized. But even the slackers and fledgling pirates pose a threat much worse than making you walk the plank.

SAFEGUARD YOUR SHIP You can make your vessel less inviting to pirates and harder to board by ringing the deck of the ship with razor wire. Fire hoses can also be installed onboard, which are helpful in a fire and quite good at spraying seawater over the side of the ship to knock boarders into the drink. You can turn your main cabin into a panic room with a solid steel door that can be barred from the inside, and a rudder control that allows you to disable steering. Some vessels have a distinctive pirate alarm, like an incredibly loud car alarm, that can be sounded in the event of attack. Other creative measures have included merchant vessels positioning mannequins on deck dressed to look like armed guards and launching flares at approaching aggressors.

THE STATS

235 Approximate number of sea piracy incidents that took place in 2014.

44 Estimated captive ship crew members held by pirates (26 were abducted in 2014).

72% Percentage of pirate attacks that occur on anchored ships.

$9.5 MILLION Cost of the highest ransom ever paid for a seized ship, the *MT Samho Dream*, which was captured off the Horn of Africa in 2010.

$16 BILLION Average cost of piracy worldwide each year, including actual losses, security costs, and shipping route changes.

40% Percentage of 2004 pirate attacks that occurred in the Strait of Malacca (ranked as the most dangerous sea route by the International Maritime Bureau).

200–600 Number of ships that cross the Strait of Malacca daily.

Somali pirates off the coast of Africa, Brazilian pirates on the Amazon, Serbian pirates on the Danube. Modern piracy is big business. On average, piracy results in an estimated worldwide loss of 16 billion USD per year. And of the violence done against seafarers, hostage-taking dominates the list of crimes perpetrated by pirates. Here are some ways to prevent these attacks and fight back.

REPEL BOARDERS Detecting small boats and potential threats is the first step against piracy. Larger craft can be picked up on radar, but small craft may avoid detection. However, newer specialized systems are using shorter wavelengths of radar, and these may pick up small boats approaching. Once detected, high-powered optics can be used to view the approaching craft and make a judgment about their intent. If you suspect they might be pirates, then use the defenses at hand. As mentioned already, razor wire and water cannons can help to repel a boarding party. Larger ships may carry very specialized defenses, such as curtains of scalding hot water or electrically charged water that the pirates would have to pass through in order to advance. Fortifying the bridge against gunfire is another great strategy, and it gives the crew a haven where they can retreat in the event of a pirate boarding.

COMMUNICATION IS KEY In the event that you are booted off your own bridge, it's not a bad idea to have a second radio hidden onboard your vessel. This could be used to reach out to the Coast Guard or to other authorities for assistance. A satellite phone could perform a similar task, allowing you to make distress calls, and it's even portable. This sat phone would need to be in a smart place, where you could reach it in a pinch but the bad guys wouldn't find it.

CONSIDER A CONVOY There is strength in numbers, and a convoy might just be the ticket to get you through pirate-infested waters. More ships means more manpower and more defenses, two things that pirates do not want to see. Coordinating a group may lengthen your voyage, but it's better to get there slower than to not get there at all.

CAN'T DO WITHOUT

ANTI-PIRACY DEVICES The laws vary, but generally speaking, recreational and merchant vessels are not allowed to carry weapons. The U.S. government, however, modified the rules in response to the rise in modern piracy. It's now possible for a U.S.-flagged ship to carry armed private security personnel. This change has inspired a new type of private security company, specializing in the protection of ships, crews, and cargo. If you choose to sail without guards, there is another option: Some super-yachts are now being equipped with special lasers that are effective up to 2.5 miles (4 km), and cause disorientation and temporary blindness at close range.

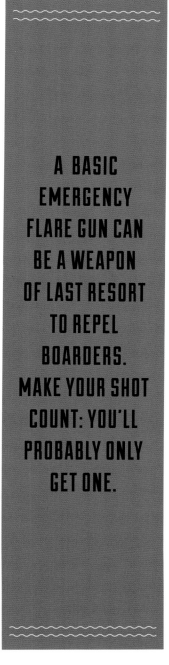

A BASIC EMERGENCY FLARE GUN CAN BE A WEAPON OF LAST RESORT TO REPEL BOARDERS. MAKE YOUR SHOT COUNT: YOU'LL PROBABLY ONLY GET ONE.

CRUISE SHIP ATTACK On October 7, 1985, four pirates took over the MS *Achille Lauro* cruise liner. The incident happened off the coast of Alexandria, Egypt, as the Italian ship was en route to Ashdod, Israel. This act of piracy was motivated more by politics than financial gain. During the event, wheelchair-bound 69-year-old American Leon Klinghoffer was murdered and thrown into the Mediterranean. U.S. President Ronald Reagan had Special Operations Forces on standby to free the vessel from its captors, but after two days of negotiations, the pirates left the ship in exchange for safe passage.

CASTAWAY

PALM-LINED BEACHES AND TROPICAL BLUE WATERS MAY SOUND LIKE A DREAM GETAWAY, BUT BEING MAROONED ON AN ISLAND COULD QUICKLY BECOME THE STUFF OF NIGHTMARES AS THE CRUSHING LONELINESS, THE DANGER OF STARVATION, AND THE FEAR OF NEVER BEING RESCUED SET IN.

After a maritime emergency, survivors in their right minds will crave help from the civilized world and do everything they can to obtain it. But what if that help is quite literally nowhere in sight?

The oceans are the Earth's greatest wilderness. Beautiful, but merciless, throughout history they have chewed sailors up and spit them out on lonely shores. Left to fend for themselves, these lost souls have had to scavenge, improvise, or do without in order to stay alive. If injury and disease aren't a factor, their lives will revolve around three inescapable tasks: finding food, collecting fresh water, and signaling for rescue.

In some cases, these shipwrecked seamen and waylaid travelers had to survive for months or even years to finally seize their chance for rescue. Could this still happen today? In fact, there are still remote corners of the globe where humans seldom tread. These are the desolate places where the missing can stay that way, until help arrives or they lose the fight.

FIND AN ISLAND If bad luck has left you adrift on the ocean, there are a few signs that can help you navigate toward land (assuming you have a paddle or a way to steer your raft). Scan the horizon for any hint of land, but don't be fooled—grayish spots on the edge of the horizon are probably just clouds or cloud shadows. Greenish spots should be land. At night, look for lights that might indicate human habitation.

In addition, keep an eye out for vegetation. Seaweed can grow in "forests" close to land, and fresh plant leaves may be seen in floating the water. Birds can help too, as they often fly away from land in the morning and toward it again in the evening. Be aware of subtle changes in currents and any new sounds such as surf.

18 YEARS Greatest period of time spent alone on a deserted island, by Juana Maria, the sole inhabitant of San Nicolas Island from 1835 to 1853.

16 MONTHS Longest time a single person was lost at sea: José Alvarenga of Mexico drifted alone for 8,000 miles (12,875 km) before reaching land.

0.9% Maximum percentage of salt in water that humans can safely drink without dehydration or other ill effects. (Seawater is 3.6% salt.)

539,000 Estimated number of deserted islands in the world.

1,404 MILES (2,260 KM) Distance between Bouvet Island, the most remote desert island, and human habitation at Tristan da Cunha in the South Atlantic (itself the most remote inhabited island on Earth).

Surviving on an island can go a lot of different ways. The majority of this section assumes that you are alone, and stuck on some tropical island. But you could just as easily be stranded with a group on an icy speck of land near the Arctic Circle. If you do end up on an island, for your sake, I hope it's warm and lush.

ASSESS YOUR NEW HOME While a lot of people mix up the terms "desert isle" and "deserted isle," they can be quite different things. A desert isle is little more than a sandbar in the sea, and very inhospitable to life. Sure, it may have rocks, sand, and a few crabs running around, but these landforms are generally bereft of fresh water and have limited or no vegetation. On the other hand, the deserted isle may be desert terrain, but it may also be a lush island covered with vegetation. It just happens to be devoid of people—that is, until you washed up. Though it is possible to survive on desert isles, and numerous sailors have done so for short periods, you're unlikely to last very long on one.

ISLAND SURVIVAL You shouldn't be shocked after reading this far into the book that the priorities of surviving on an island are virtually the same as if you were lost in a mountainous wilderness or derelict in the desert. Your "survival priorities" still start off with shelter, unless there is a pressing medical issue that needs attention. Next you'd need fresh water, the great irony of the castaway who's stranded on an island surrounded by undrinkable saltwater. Making fire, locating food, and signaling for rescue are important tasks as well. Defense from dangerous island fauna may make your list too.

SET UP SHELTER You still need shelter, even in the tropics. As unlikely as it seems, you can still die of hypothermia on your warm tropical refuge. If temperatures drop and you're soaked by bone-chilling rain, hypothermia can kill you in a day or two. Shelter also plays a role in your safety by getting you up off the ground. In tropical climates, dangerous snakes, spiders, insects, and other creatures take over the ground at night. A raised bed or platform gets you out of

CAN'T DO WITHOUT

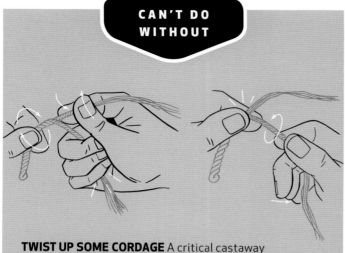

TWIST UP SOME CORDAGE A critical castaway commodity is rope, and it's actually quite easy to make. Start by collecting the strongest fibers you can find. This may be coconut husk fiber, palm leaf strips, or the fibrous inner bark from numerous plants and trees. Grab a small length of this material and begin twisting it. Continue twisting until it kinks. Hold the kink, and keep twisting each bundle of fiber. If you twisted clockwise to begin the cord, then keep twisting the fiber bundles clockwise, allowing them to encircle each other counterclockwise. When one of the two "legs" of fiber starts running out, it's time to splice in more material to that section. Use a new fiber bundle that is the same thickness as the one that's ending. Taper the ends of the new and old bundle, so that they both end at a point. Intermingle the fibers from both bundles and continue twisting your rope.

their path and into a safer location. Any kind of material that can act as a mosquito net will be invaluable when used with this raised platform. Failing that, keep a smoky fire burning upwind from your shack to act as a bug-repelling smudge. Cone-shaped shelters are best, since they shed heavy rain better than other architectural shapes. Palm leaves, as well as fig and banana leaves, make ideal roofing

≈≈ T/F ≈≈

THERE AREN'T ANY UNMAPPED ISLANDS LEFT TO FIND

TRUE, AS FAR AS WE KNOW With the implementation of global satellite mapping, there isn't a corner of the globe that hasn't been peered at and mapped. This doesn't mean that the maps are accurate to tiny details, like miniscule isles and sandbars. It may well be that in the less-traveled parts of the Pacific, tiny islands may be mapped inaccurately or not at all. The other point to consider is the rapid rate of change for small landmasses. One good typhoon may wash away small sandy islands, while the current piles up sand to create new ones.

materials. And remember to avoid building your shelter under coconut trees. A coconut falling on your head from a height of 50 feet (15 m) could be fatal! One person gets killed by a coconut every couple of years, worldwide.

FINDING FRESH WATER If your new island residence is a flat and empty patch of sand, then locating fresh water may be your biggest hurdle to survival. In those dire conditions, praying for rain may be your best hope. That and the odd coconut washed up on the beach may be your only drinking water sources. In sharp contrast, a larger island tends to be abundant in fresh water. Look for small streams or larger waterways running down to the beach, and boil the water to disinfect it. Caves may have water dripping inside them, and you could even try digging a well. Larger islands tend to create cloud formations above them, which can help you spot them at a distance and generate ample rainfall. Thunderstorms provide a lot of water quickly, so set out plenty of containers to collect this free fresh water. But whatever you do, remember that drinking seawater will kill you, unless you can make a solar still to desalinate it.

FOOD Even a barren sandbar can be laden with food, if you know where to look. Most species of mollusks, oysters, clams, mussels, seaweed, and fish can be eaten safely, though keep in mind that there are always a few poisonous ones out there. If you have fire as a tool, then use it to cook your foraged foods to kill parasites, bacteria, and other pathogens that it may contain. Larger islands often have numerous bird species, which can be a source of meat and eggs. You may even get lucky and find some feral livestock. It's not uncommon for ships to carry goats, sheep, pigs, and other animals, which can become naturalized on islands after they're shipwrecked or released there.

COOK WITH ROCKS Lacking the cooking equipment that the average traveler might carry, a marooned survivor will have to improvise an effective way to cook her food. A great way to do this is by cooking on a hot flat rock. This stone should be one that can handle high heat, and not be

FOR A DIY SUNSCREEN, CRUSH SOME FATTY COCONUT MEAT AND APPLY IT LIBERALLY TO YOUR SKIN. YOU'LL GET SOME UV PROTECTION, AND YOU'LL SMELL FANTASTIC!

GOOD TO KNOW

THE PERFECT FOOD?
You could live off coconuts. And if you're not convinced, ask Michael Mangal. He was stranded on an island in India's Andaman archipelago after the 2005 tsunami. Mangal survived 25 days on coconuts before being rescued. Green coconuts are a good source of drinkable water, holding about 12 ounces each.

Mature brown coconuts provide about 500 calories each, due to high fat content. The oily meat of these fuzzy brown orbs is high in potassium and many other minerals. It can be eaten raw, grated and pressed to make coconut milk, or diced up and cooked. Coconuts contain lauric acid, a fatty acid also found in human breast milk. This acid supports the immune system, and it's both antibacterial and antiviral.

too gritty or rough, as the food will stick to it. Fish, clams, seaweed, and chunks of coconut will go down a lot easier if they are cooked by frying. The rock griddle can be greased with coconut oil and propped up on a stand of rocks, or it can straddle a trench in the dirt with the fire underneath. Maintain a coal bed under your griddle, and feed it plenty of twigs, sticks, or pieces of coconut husk.

Some rocks are not very heat-resistant, and may pop or crumble. Test unfamiliar rocks by placing them in a large fire and moving far away in case they start flinging out superheated shards. Never get rocks from a wet location, as they can explode when heated.

Look for a flattish stone with a slight depression in its surface, to better hold your oil. Proper frying requires fairly high heat, so be sure your fire is strong and you have a good supply of fuel before you start making your DIY fishsticks.

GOOD TO KNOW

MAKE A FISH SPEAR

A time-rich island survivalist needs a hobby (and a way to score some tasty fish). Crafting a fish spear can take care of both items. If all you have is driftwood, pick out the most spear-like piece you can find. An island with woody trees and similar vegetation may give you plenty of choices. Try to find one that forks or split the stick to create a fork.

Carve and sharpen these forked tips, and attach a sharp spike in between them. Use the spear by stalking carefully through the water, with the spear's tip already under the surface. When a promising seafood target is spotted, aim below the fish to allow for the refraction of light, and thrust. With any luck, the fish has been pierced by one of the three sharp spear points and you have fish for dinner.

SIGNALING A signaling strategy is your surest ticket to being rescued. To maximize your chances, build large signal fires on prominent hills and other high-visibility locations. Try your hand at creating flags out of scavenged materials. Charcoal powder can make flags jet black, which is a great contrast against white sandy beaches. Whichever signals you make, make them large and make an effort. You do want your ship to come in, right?

SAVE YOUR SANITY For a person stranded all alone, one of the hardest survival issues may be maintaining good mental health. Mental issues should not be surprising, as few humans fare well in isolation. Most of us crave a little solitude from time to time, but it's occasional and voluntary. A long-term solo survival experience is neither. These conditions are likely to erode the mental and emotional well-being of the survivor, and cause him to become enormously disturbed.

Aggressiveness, anxiety, paranoia, obsessive thoughts, hallucinations, and suicidal actions have been documented in cases where a person has been deprived of close social and physical contact. How can you cope with these potentially devastating circumstances? Survivors have had good luck maintaining some semblance of mental health by finding a higher meaning in their predicament, by anthropomorphizing inanimate objects (talking to your friend the volleyball), and by considering wild animals to be your pets.

SALVAGE SOMETHING USEFUL A downed plane or broken-up boat may be the reason you're the new monarch of your wild island. These wrecked craft may also be the source of items that aid you in your survival. Wreckage can give you materials that can be used for shelters, beds, water catches, tools, and weapons, as well as food, clothing, and medicine. Use your imagination and let the creativity flow as you make things that assist your survival. You may not be able to whip up a coconut radio like the Professor did on Gilligan's Island, but you can certainly find ways to make your island life more tolerable.

A Real-Life Castaway

For the ultimate story of island survival, look no further than the story of Alexander Selkirk, the Scottish sailor who survived four years as a castaway. Selkirk was reportedly the inspiration behind Daniel Defoe's novel *Robinson Crusoe*. In 1704, Selkirk was a sailor serving under Captain Thomas Stradling. After a supply stop in the middle of their South Pacific expedition, the captain and Selkirk had a disagreement about the safety of their voyage with the extra weight they now carried.

After Selkirk tried to rally the crew against the captain, Stradling decided to maroon Selkirk by himself on the island of Juan Fernández. Selkirk proved to be a hardy survivor, building a shelter near the shore in hopes that he could signal a passing ship. Selkirk initially lived on oysters, shellfish, and any other sea creatures he could catch.

Eventually, he traveled deeper into the jungle island and captured a few feral goats. These provided him with milk, meat, and hides for clothing. He also managed to attract a few feral cats, which guarded him from rat bites while he slept. On February 1, 1709, Selkirk was finally rescued by a passing ship, four years and four months after his former captain abandoned him.

HUNTED LIKE PREY

YOUR PULSE POUNDS IN YOUR EARS AS YOUR FEET POUND THE GROUND. YOU HAVE TO GET AWAY, BUT WHERE CAN YOU HIDE? YOU'RE BEING HUNTED BY THE MOST CLEVER PREDATOR ON EARTH: MAN. IT DOESN'T MATTER WHY THEY'RE AFTER YOU; ALL THAT MATTERS NOW IS ESCAPE.

We modern folks may enjoy the trappings of civilization—we may even think of ourselves as highly evolved. But at our core, we still bear the animalistic drives of our distant ancestors. Ruled by hunger and instinct, rather than codes and law, our progenitors were free to do as they pleased—even to hunt each other. Contemporary fiction has tapped into this dark past, with books and movies about people hunting each other for sport or as part of some futuristic game show.

In fact, closer to home, this type of human behavior isn't restricted to the realm of fiction and fantasy. All you have to do is listen to the stories of soldiers and law enforcement personnel who have been hunted by others. These are some of the most chilling tales you could ever hear, and the worst part is that they are true. Just as truth is stranger than fiction, it can also be deadlier. These pursuers, abductors, and killers display the depravity of the worst people on earth and plumb the lowest depths of the human soul.

DEFEAT BOTH MAN AND BEAST

There's a reason bloodhounds (more properly called "scent dogs") strike fear into the hearts of criminals. The fact is, if you're hunted by men with a scent dog, the odds will never be in your favor, and those tricks you've seen in the movies won't work.. But you may still get away, if you can cast doubt into dog handler's mind.

If you have some distance between you and your pursuers, take a minute to run back and forth in different directions over a 15-yard (14-m) area. Then run away on a very different bearing than you were last headed. The dog will follow your scent in the crazy pattern, leading your pursuer to doubt the dog and believe it has lost the scent. Make him question the dog, and you may get away.

THE STATS

250 Claimed number of homicides committed by Mafia hitman Richard Kuklinski, also known as "The Iceman."

$200,000 Down payment for a contract killing paid to undercover investigator Gary Johnson by a socialite to have her husband murdered.

80 Average number of yearly murder-for-hire cases handled undercover by the FBI.

461 YEARS Duration of prison sentence (plus a life sentence) for Alaskan serial killer Robert C. Hansen, who abducted and hunted at least 17 women in a "Deadliest Game" scenario.

2,707 YARDS (2,475 M) Distance of longest confirmed sniper kill, by British soldier Craig Harrison, in Afghanistan in 2009.

36 HOURS Maximum age of a scent trail that a bloodhound can find.

ESCAPE ON FOOT Getting away on foot has everything to do with your location. Perhaps you stumbled upon a backwoods meth lab, and you're being hunted in a wilderness area. Your best bet is to make a break for civilization. You don't want to linger in the wild, because there is a decided lack of witnesses out there. You could get caught and end up as fertilizer under some drug cartel's marijuana plants. Escape from pursuers in an urban environment is a very different scenario. You'll need to blend into the crowd, move quickly but not quickly enough to create a disturbance, and make your way to a safe haven. Police stations are great sanctuaries, but they're few and far between. Hopping into a yellow cab in a sea of yellow cabs might be the best choice you'll have.

KILLER CAMOUFLAGE Want to disappear? If you can't escape your hunters in the wild and you don't have a ghillie suit (the rag suit worn by military snipers), then make the next best thing—a mud suit. We've seen versions of it in action flicks, and shockingly, it's a legitimate and effective camouflage technique. The first step is to wallow in some mud, coating every square inch of your body, clothing optional. Then roll on the ground to pick up leaves, moss, and bits of debris. Whether crouched in the bushes, lying flat on the ground, or just standing there pretending to be a stump—this highly effective camouflage will allow you to completely disappear.

ESCAPE A CAR CHASE The classic vehicle chase of the entertainment industry has nothing to do with a car chase in real life. If you're driving and being pursued, you'll have two choices in front of you: continue driving or flee on foot. If you're a speedy runner and you have your running shoes on, this may be your best option. If you're not so spry, then keep driving. If you can get out of your pursuer's view for a few seconds, you may be able to pull into a hidden spot somewhere, or change direction and lose them.

EVASIVE DRIVING MANEUVERS One of the best (or at least one of the coolest) evasive driving tricks is the bootlegger's

GOOD TO KNOW

CHANGE UP YOUR LOOK This isn't the stylish kind of makeover that would be featured on a television show, but the streetwise kind that might just save your life.

STEP 1 Change your main color scheme. Color plays a major role in hunting, as it has for millennia. Change the color on the upper half of your body by ditching your jacket or finding another garment. Human predators will be confused and potentially still looking for the wrong color.

STEP 2 Change your head. People look at faces and heads for recognition. Put on eyeglasses or sunglasses. Ditch your hat, add a hat, or don some different headwear. Change your hair, if you don't have a hat.

STEP 3 Change your behavior. Predators are expecting their prey to run away, so do the opposite. Modify your appearance and find a place to blend in. Sit down with strangers and get them talking, walk toward your hunters (head down, don't make eye contact, fiddle with your phone like everyone else), or do something else unexpected and counterintuitive.

turn. This driving maneuver can be traced back to the Prohibition Era, when moonshiners would get out of view of the chasing police, and make a complete 180-degree turn in the road. The point of the trick is to confuse pursuers, who wouldn't believe a car could turn around that quickly. This is best done in a car with a foot emergency brake, and the brake-release handle should be taped in the open position so it won't lock. Drop your speed to 40 miles per hour (64 kph), and do two things at once. Stand on your emergency brake and turn the steering wheel all the way to your left. When the car has slid most of the way through the turn, let off of the emergency brake and straighten out your wheel. Then floor the accelerator and drive past your pursuers. The Duke boys would be so proud of you.

T / F

MAN IS THE DEADLIEST ANIMAL ON EARTH

FALSE In fact, we don't even come close. It's the littlest of creatures that do the most killing. No species, including *Homo sapiens*, is responsible for more loss of human life than mosquitoes and the pathogens in dirty water. The World Health Organization estimates that 3.4 million people die annually from water-related microbial diseases. Mosquitoes carrying malaria are the next worst, killing approximately 600,000 people each year. Add in other ailments, and the mosquito death toll climbs to 725,000.

SOCIAL COLLAPSE

GONE IS THE CIVILITY OF MODERN LIFE AND GONE IS THE ENFORCEMENT OF LAW. YOUR MILD-MANNERED SLICE OF SUBURBIA OR YOUR PLEASANT UPSCALE URBAN NEIGHBORHOOD IS NOW A HELLHOLE BESET WITH ROBBERY, LOOTING, VANDALISM, MURDER, AND DESPAIR.

Welcome to the end of the world as we know it (and nobody feels fine). In fact, the worst has happened, everything we took for granted is vanishing, or lies in ruins at our feet. Although you may not want to face the awful truth, you can't say that you weren't warned. Even though all those alarmists seemed like a bunch of nut jobs, sooner or later it became clear that they were onto something.

This is a frightening scenario to even contemplate, let alone prepare for. The collapse of society would be a total nightmare, almost literally unthinkable to most modern people. So they spend their days *not* thinking about it. They ignore the warnings, the second chances, and the opportunities to change their paths. Then one day, finally, the first domino tips and starts to fall. The unstoppable chain reaction of our culture's demise begins, and none can escape it.

The collapse of society is the sum of all the reasons that preppers prepare, but are they even ready for this?

DO WE REALLY HAVE TO WORRY?

You're reading a book filled with some pretty unsettling (and some folks would say, unlikely) content, so something is obviously on your mind. But what's your next move: panic, worry, or denial? Let me stop you before you answer "panic." Even when the worst has occurred, there have always been survivors. The fall of the Roman Empire didn't mean that every single Roman dropped dead. It meant that one way of life drifted into something else.

Even when civilizations have ended with catastrophic loss of life, many people found ways to survive. They changed, and became a new culture. So worry a little, but don't panic or live in denial. Remember that change is the only constant.

THE STATS

15,000 Population of Rome in the 9th century C.E. (compared to its former 1.5 million in the 2nd century) following the collapse of the Roman Empire.

53% Percentage of American households without a three-day supply of food and water.

$100 TRILLION The largest—and still virtually worthless—denomination on a banknote of currency during the height of hyperinflation in 2008 in Zimbabwe.

THE MATRIX

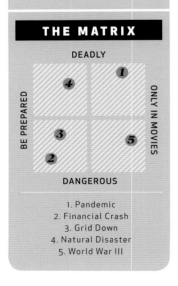

DEADLY

BE PREPARED

ONLY IN MOVIES

DANGEROUS

1. Pandemic
2. Financial Crash
3. Grid Down
4. Natural Disaster
5. World War III

PREPARE OR REACT? There are great arguments to be made both for making massive preparations and for only making a few preps in the face of a civilization collapse. The mega-preppers with their food hoard in a bunker are very well situated for most disasters and scenarios where things are unhinged for a long time. They'd be fat and happy after a lengthy societal collapse, as long as no one found them or their stash. The biggest problems with this plan are the expense of these preparations and the fact that the stockpile is typically not mobile. In events where evacuation is necessary, these mega-preppers are not much better off than the apartment-dwelling bug-out prepper — that is, they are limited to what they can carry.

The other side of this whole coin is someone who is not focused on stockpiling, but instead on being adaptable and able to react quickly to a specific disaster once she knows what's going on. This reactive person focuses on training rather than hoarding, and is highly mobile. Which prepping style would "win" in a collapse scenario? I'd say you need a little bit of both. Those food stocks could get you through a long cold winter. I don't care how good your skills are—you can't make food appear where there is none. And being more skilled, rather than just being a hoarder, can give you the flexibility to make moves and potentially stay safer than a fixed target.

THE TRIGGERS This book is jam-packed with scenarios that could potentially trigger a collapse of civilization. Here are a few of the triggers, and what to do in each situation.

As we discuss elsewhere in this book, a pandemic is a major concern. Isolation from the infected would be your first concern in surviving a collapse by disease. You'd have to make it through the initial wave of illness to be able to wade through the subsequent collapse. Then you'll have to keep yourself from getting infected as you shift into a survival lifestyle, until the disease has run its course.

By contrast, in a financial crash, at least no one's dropping dead from the super-flu . . . but the dollar has likely died. Crime and shortages of necessities are the biggest issues here. You'll want ample means to defend

CAN'T DO WITHOUT

BICYCLE Whether it's a street cruiser or a mountain bike, a bicycle will keep working as long as you have strength to pedal it. A bicycle doesn't need gasoline, electricity, or a functional financial system to operate. All it needs is you. Add a few accessories like a basket or pannier packs, and now you can even carry small loads. Just be painfully aware that you'll be the envy of the neighborhood, and this may attract unwanted attention. Also consider that it's unbelievably easy to kick someone off a bike. All an envious fellow survivor needs to do is kick the bike (or your body) as you zip past them, and down you go. You're injured, the bike is taken, and you start crying. It's fourth grade all over again. Except last time it happened, your parents got the bike back. This time, you're on your own.

yourself, and a stock of everything you might need to ride out the first few months of a financial collapse. After that, you'll have to figure out a new way to live. Maybe you'll run into a guy named Max and he can direct you to Bartertown.

Next up? Power problems. Whether by EMP, hackers, solar flare, or something altogether unforeseen, the power grid goes down and so does the tech-dependent modern

T / F

A NASA STUDY SAYS SOCIETY IS ABOUT TO COLLAPSE

TRUE A recent study partly sponsored by NASA has projected the collapse of global industrial civilization within the next few decades. The study is filled with examples of the recurring global cycle of rise-and-collapse showing that no matter how advanced or complex the socioeconomic system was, they all had to end sometime. That said, the study's authors did offer a sliver of hope. They suggested that collapse could be avoided if the depletion of nature fell to a sustainable level, and if the gap between the rich and the poor was lessened.

T / F

DURING A SOCIETAL COLLAPSE, HEAD FOR A REMOTE FARM

FALSE A farm is a target, especially to hungry people. Even the most clueless urbanite knows that food comes from farms. Another reason to avoid the remote farm scene is the isolation. If there is still any law enforcement left, they won't be in the remote areas. This turns any out-of-the-way locale into a lawless no-man's-land. Don't believe it? Just look up the Salvadoran Civil War. A friend who lived through it said that roving gangs wandered the outlying countryside, targeting farms and killing with impunity. This went on for almost a decade.

lifestyle. Hope you stocked up on candles and the know-how to live an 1800s-style life. Hand tools, manual labor, and non-electric items would be key to survival without the warm glow of electricity.

Somewhat related is the specter of a truly catastrophic natural disaster. This can happen through a number of disasters, the worst of which would be a one-two punch. An earthquake devastates an area and sets off a nearby volcano. Most people and relief organizations can deal with one disaster, but two of them at the same time and in the same region could be unmanageable.

Finally, there's always that angry horseman, War. A modern global conflict (WWIII) would send the world into chaos and likely trigger a number of smaller (yet still dangerous) events. Terrorism associated with war could include bio-terrorism, which would have localized effects similar to an epidemic. Electrical grids could be attacked and shut down. And based on the war theater and where you live, you could even be caught in the crossfire. An out-of-the-way locale is your best bet to survive the mayhem that a contemporary world war would unleash.

BUILD A NETWORK No matter how the fall comes, surviving it will mean starting to rebuild. Any trusted friends and family who have made it through the "crash" will be the basis of your survival network. No doubt, these folks will be a diverse group with a varied assortment of skill sets. Don't rule out anybody trustworthy. You'd be surprised what people can accomplish when they have to do something. The elders in the group can offer their wisdom and experience, and they'll have a lifetime of skills to draw upon. The kids can be easily trained to do important tasks, since their young minds are so adept at learning. Friend-of-a-friend types and newcomers could be valuable too, but they'll have to prove themselves. After a collapse, you can't just trust everybody.

Structure your inner network like the military for best results. Work in teams, watch each other's backs, be prepared to defend each other, and maintain a clear chain of command. Everyone needs to know their job.

SCAVENGE FOR THE UNEXPECTED While all the twentysomethings are looting the drugstore and killing each other for Vicodin, you're better off looking for food and other vital supplies in unorthodox locations. Pay a visit to the hamburger joints that keep 50-pound (23-kg) sacks of potatoes lying out in the eating area, and the Italian eateries that keep large jugs of olive oil on the wall.

If things are still somewhat civil, maybe try to buy or barter for these caloric resources. And if not, well, you've got to do what you've got to do. But whatever you do, don't go to the grocery store if people are looting and killing each other there. If you didn't prepare for this situation, try to find places that would have useful supplies and food that no one else would think about.

Over time, your network may expand its relationships. You may gain trading partners. These people should not be trusted as you trust your inner network, but you'll need to extend a little trust to build new contacts. You may also try to add "tradesmen" to your list of semi-trusted people who you have dealings with. These people could be doctors, dentists, farmers, hunters, craftsmen, or anybody who can provide something that your own network cannot. Make sure you play your cards close to the chest with these semi-trusted people. They don't need to know how many people are in your group, how much food you have, or any other details that you need to keep secret.

BUILD A DEFENSIVE PERIMETER After a crash, you won't be in a position to build a compound, block walls, or guard towers. But you can make the area you're in more secure and more defensible. First, you'll have to decide what you are willing to defend. Mark the boundaries of your protected area, and use existing barriers like walls, waterways, buildings, and fences to help define your territory. Next, set a controlled entry/exit point for the area. This could be one exterior door on a building, while most others are boarded up. This may mean blocking off a street with vehicles, if they are operational.

ENHANCE YOUR DEFENSES This can be anything from locking gates in fences, to boarding up windows and doors around the perimeter. Look at your perimeter from the outside, try to figure out ways in, and do your best to seal them off. Then, figure out your fallback position—where you'd retreat to within your perimeter. Keep it well supplied with water and food, and make sure there is an exit from that position in case of siege.

CREATE OBSERVATION POSTS Observation posts are the eyes and ears of your defensive perimeter. Set up OPs on outside corners of buildings or fences, as these could allow one guard to see down two perpendicular walls or fence rows. Favor high positions and defensible spots when picking OPs, and make sure there is an escape route that offers your guard a safe, quick exit. Communications are a must at the OP. The observation post is useless if the guards cannot communicate what they are seeing. If two-way radios are available and functional, they can be vital to communication. Cell phones would work too, if the system is still operational.

PREPARE FOR FIRES Many collapse scenarios could result in unchecked fires sweeping through both wilderness and urban areas. With the fire department likely disbanded in the collapse, you'll need to keep fire prevention as a high priority in your network. Keep fire extinguishers handy, limit candle use and trash fires if possible, and choose some of your group to act as firefighters. If there is no water pressure to spray garden hoses on a fire, then grab buckets and form an old-fashioned bucket line from a water source to the fire.

WHEN THERE ARE NO MORE POLICE, YOU HAVE TO BE YOUR OWN SECURITY FORCE. TAKE THIS RESPONSIBILITY SERIOUSLY AND REMAIN VIGILANT.

The End of Easter Island

*E*aster Island (Rapa Nui) is an island in the South Pacific, most commonly known for its iconic "giant head" statues called *moai*. These unique statues were a massive engineering feat—some are more than 13 feet (4 m) tall and weigh more than 14 tons (12,700 kg).

What is less commonly known about Rapa Nui is the collapse of its population over the 17th century, when it fell from 15,000 to around 2,000. European diseases and Peruvian slave raids continued over the following century, until the population fell as low as 111 in 1877.

Historical and archaeological evidence points to disease, famine, civil war, slave raids, the near deforestation of the island, and even cannibalism as reasons for the decline. While disease and slaving took the heaviest toll, deforestation played a slow and sinister role. The lack of large trees meant the end of boat production, which significantly impacted the fishing activities of the island's inhabitants and prevented their escape from the island.

The Easter Island civilization collapsed due to overpopulation, overconsumption of natural resources, disease, and attacks from outside their culture. This sad story can perhaps serve as a cautionary tale for our times.

DEATH FROM ABOVE

IT'S EASY TO IMAGINE THE BLACKNESS OF SPACE BEING FILLED WITH PERILS. SOME THREATS ARE REAL, VETTED BY SCIENCE AND FACT. OTHERS MAY EXIST ONLY IN SCI-FI. BUT IF WE'VE LEARNED ANYTHING FROM MOVIES, IT'S THAT IN SPACE, NO ONE CAN HEAR YOU SCREAM.

Space may be the final frontier, but it can also send you to your final destination. It's entirely possible (yet immensely improbable) that you could get clobbered by a piece of space trash, a meteorite, or a crashing alien spacecraft, when you're walking out your door. Okay, maybe not the last one (unless your home is somewhere near Area 51), but the others have really happened. And the fact is that not every danger presented in this category has a survival solution.

A dinosaur-exterminating asteroid strike, like the one that hit Earth 66 million years ago, is game over for everyone. But other situations may allow us a fighting chance to survive. A massive asteroid strike, or a plague caused by an alien pathogen, or most other space-related scenarios, leave you needing the same survival necessities that other situations require.

You need shelter, water, food, first aid, and security from hazards. And this generally doesn't change much, regardless of the situation.

ALIENS? REALLY? There's no way to write a book like this, with a section like this, and not mention the "A" word. That's right, aliens. Whether you're a true believer, obsessed with alien conspiracy cover-up TV shows and a crop circle of your very own out back, or you wouldn't believe even if a little green alien kicked you, you have to allow one fact. It's impossible to prove that there's *not* other life out there.

And if there is intelligent life somewhere, what are the chances they'd be friendly? If Earth's history is any guide, when one culture discovers another culture that's technologically inferior, it doesn't go so well for the low-tech people. Hide your precious metals and supermodels! Mars may not need women, but the slug people of Hexalon 7 just might.

THE STATS

500 Estimated number of meteorites that reach Earth's surface each year.

1 IN 700,000 Chance of being killed by an asteroid impact.

12% Odds of a potentially Earth-damaging solar flare happening before 2022. (One barely missed us in 2012.)

3,000 LIGHT YEARS Minimum estimated distance of a gamma ray burst that reached Earth in 774 C.E.—a closer event would likely have meant our extinction.

THE MATRIX

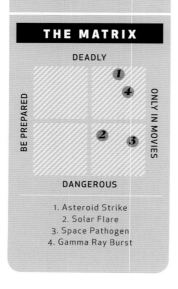

DEADLY

BE PREPARED

ONLY IN MOVIES

DANGEROUS

1. Asteroid Strike
2. Solar Flare
3. Space Pathogen
4. Gamma Ray Burst

Ask any astronaut about space and they'll tell you it is dark, and full of terrors. While space can be a fascinating topic, it's also quite easy for it to be a backdrop for fearful things. Given that space is so inhospitable to human life, it only makes sense that we would associate some dread with it. There are even a few things out there worth dreading.

ASTEROID STRIKE Asteroids, comets, and meteors can hurtle through our atmosphere at astonishing speeds and strike the ground with unbelievable force.

It's believed that a huge asteroid struck the Earth millions of years ago, triggering global cooling and wiping out the dinosaurs. The massive Tunguska asteroid strike in 1908 was the largest recorded explosion of a space object, estimated to rival a 10 megaton blast or greater. And more recently, on February 15, 2013, a meteor exploded over Russia's Ural Mountains. The sonic booms from this strike injured roughly 1,100 people and hospitalized 48. It doesn't take a very big piece of rock to do a lot of damage. Just a 30-foot (10-m) object can impact with the same energy as a nuclear bomb. Is it possible to neutralize the threat of a strike? Yes, and that's why scientists are monitoring near

IF THE POLES SHIFT, IT WOULD BE A WORLD-ENDING CATASTROPHE

FALSE The magnetic poles are always creeping into new positions. But can they swing wildly and violently to distant, new points? Not likely. According to NASA, the Earth's magnetic poles reverse every 200,000 to 300,000 years. And although we are overdue for the next one, these magnetic shifts happen slowly, taking hundreds or thousands of years. During this process (which has happened many times before), multiple magnetic poles may emerge at strange new latitudes, but it's hardly an extinction event— just confusing to migrating birds.

Earth objects, and tracking their paths through space. The hope is that we can nuke an incoming rock before it nukes us. I hope they're right.

SOLAR FLARE The sun is not only a source of light and warmth for the earth, it also creates flares that could mean big trouble for our tech-dependent world. There are three classes of solar eruptions. Class "C" flares, which are the weakest, really don't do anything. Class "M" flares, which are moderate, give us more radiation and particles than a "C." They are responsible for the Northern Lights traveling outside their normal territories. Then there are Class "X" flares. These are strong enough to cause disruptions in satellites and communication systems here on Earth, and could potentially overload electrical grids. A huge Class "X" flare hit the Earth in 1859, the largest flare ever recorded. It created auroras worldwide and interrupted telegraph service for weeks. A similar solar storm in 1989 caused over 6 million people in Quebec to lose their electricity. How does a flare do something mischievous like that? Solar flares and storms can affect modern technology with their three different emissions: magnetic, radio, and radiation.

T/F

YOU'RE AT RISK OF GETTING HIT BY SPACE JUNK

TRUE, BUT BARELY

Although NASA has stated that there are 22,000 pieces of space debris, there has only been one legitimate case of space junk hitting a person (so far). In 1997, Oklahoma native Lottie Williams was hit in the shoulder by a small piece of blackened, woven metallic material, later confirmed to be part of a rocket fuel tank which had launched a U.S. Air Force satellite in 1996. Thankfully, Ms. Williams was not injured. NASA says that approximately one piece of space debris makes it through re-entry each year (most burns up).

The magnetic emissions have the ability to overload electrical systems. The radio emissions can obviously interfere with communications. And the radiation is probably the worst of the bunch, causing planes to reroute and endangering satellites, spacecraft, and astronauts alike. In other words, the radiation makes it a bad day to be outside, or flying in an airplane.

SPACE PATHOGENS Life can exist in space, and not just inside a space station. Numerous bacteria and plankton species from Earth have also survived the extremes of space travel. These seemingly inhospitable conditions appear to induce a sort of cryosleep in many microscopic organisms, which are all too happy to revive when they are brought into warmer and wetter conditions. This begs the question, what would happen if a microbe from some other part of the solar system hitched a ride to Earth, say in a large frosty comet? What are the chances it would be a harmful pathogen to humans, plants, or animals? There are more questions than answers here, and let's pray those questions never get answered.

GAMMA RAY BURSTS Gamma-ray bursts (or GRBs) are flashes of energy that have been observed in distant galaxies as a narrow beam of intense radiation released during a supernova or hypernova. These powerful beams can last a few milliseconds or several minutes. All of the GRBs observed to date have happened far outside our galaxy and have had no effect on us. But if a GRB were to happen within the Milky Way and we were unlucky enough to be in its path, the effects could be catastrophic. It is estimated that the average gamma ray burst would deplete much of the Earth's ozone layer, bombard the Earth's surface with radiation, and cause mass extinction and the destruction of the food chain. The gamma ray energy could possibly also cause chemical reactions in the atmosphere, creating a photochemical smog. This would darken the skies enough to create a global winter. At that point, we're pretty much a dead planet—except for roaches and bacteria, which can survive anything.

The Tunguska Event

The Tunguska asteroid strike (or Tunguska event) was a large explosion of an asteroid or comet over a wilderness area in Russia, on June 30, 1908. It's believed that the explosion occurred 3 to 6 miles (5-10 km) above the ground, based on the pattern of flattened trees over 830 square miles (2,150 sq. km) of surrounding area. This is the largest impact ever recorded, knocking down an estimated 80 million trees and creating a shock wave that would have measured 5.0 on the Richter scale. Whether asteroid or comet, several different studies have estimated that the object was between 200-620 feet (60-190 m) in size, and equal in its explosive energy to 10-15 megatons of TNT—roughly 1,000 times greater than the atomic bomb dropped on Hiroshima. It's amazingly lucky that it hit a largely unpopulated region.

ZOMBIES! RUN!

WHAT IF OUR FRIENDS AND FAMILY TURN AGAINST US? WHAT IF THEY ARE NO LONGER THEMSELVES? THEY'RE SOMETHING ELSE, HELL-BENT ON DOING US HARM. CALL THEM WHAT YOU WILL—WALKERS, ZOMBIES, LIVING DEAD. THERE IS ONLY ONE CALL THEY HEED NOW: HUNGER.

So what's the deal with zombies? You can't turn on a TV or walk through a bookstore without seeing these flesh-eating foes shambling ominously. Zombies are one of the most popular villains in sci-fi and horror. But why? I'm no psychologist, yet I have a theory.

This idea has formed from years of teaching survival skills and working with otherwise reasonable people who genuinely fear a zombie apocalypse. Why are they so scared of zombies? I think it boils down to a very basic fear.

It's natural for us to fear that the familiar will become unfamiliar, that those we once loved will somehow become a threat to us. Imagine how horrifying it really would be for your best friend to not be himself anymore. The things that formed his personality are gone. Instead, there is something that looks like him—but now it's trying to hurt you. That should scare just about anybody.

So, what are the odds it could happen? Doubtful, at best. But just in case . . .

THE VIGILANT SURVIVE Whatever the emergency, being vigilant and observant are key factors for survival. If I'm wrong (that's a big IF) and someday a zombie outbreak happens, I would treat the situation as if I were caught in any other hostile environment, like a violent riot. I'd be as observant as possible of the situation, so that I could be alert to all possible dangers. Next, I'd seek shelter in a location that could be secured from the inside.

I'd stay quiet and off the radar of potential attackers while arming myself with whatever I could scare up. And I'd try to get information from any sources available. The radio, TV, or a few quick phone calls could give me the information I'd need to make the right choices to survive.

THE STATS

14% Percentage of the American population that believes a zombie apocalypse could happen.

$5.74 BILLION Estimated economic value of zombie films and related media.

4 MPH (6.4 KPH) Top speed of a "slow" zombie in TV and movies; "fast" versions can run at speeds up to 18 mph (29 kph).

2100 B.C.E. First recorded zombie reference, found in the *Epic of Gilgamesh*.

THE MATRIX

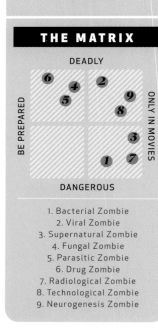

DEADLY

BE PREPARED

ONLY IN MOVIES

DANGEROUS

1. Bacterial Zombie
2. Viral Zombie
3. Supernatural Zombie
4. Fungal Zombie
5. Parasitic Zombie
6. Drug Zombie
7. Radiological Zombie
8. Technological Zombie
9. Neurogenesis Zombie

HOW IT COULD HAPPEN If you hadn't guessed already, I am a zombie nonbeliever. I'll watch a few shows about them, but I'm not convinced it will ever happen. That being said, I have to concede that there are chemicals, drugs, and other agents that could produce a zombie-like state in your friends and family members, potentially turning them against you. But there are no known pathogens or chemicals that would cause the highly contagious and highly entertaining zombie apocalypse scenario that most movies, books, and shows portray.

BUILD YOUR TEAM If you expect to make it through the zombie wars without any bite marks, you'll need a good team, not just a bunch of randoms who only last one season. Here are some skill sets to look for in your new team members.

Law enforcement and military folks have training in firearms. Hunters and shooting enthusiasts have spent some time behind the sights, too. Add them to your sharpshooting defense force.

You're also going to need medics: EMTs, doctors, nurses, dentists, and other professionals bring vital medical skills, which you'll need when the call comes through to "send more paramedics!"

You'll want to have at least a few builders on your team: handymen, MacGyvers, and jack-of-all-trades types will be absolutely priceless over the long haul, when you need to be building, fortifying, engineering, and improvising secure shelters, potable water sources, and other necessities.

Which brings us to food supply: you'll need something to eat when the canned food runs out. Anyone can become a farmer, but there's a lot to know and you can't afford the steep learning curve when everybody's starving. It's better to have skills and experience going in.

FIND A FORTRESS Once your team is set, it's time to find a new home that you can defend against the walkers. An abandoned correctional facility could be a handy base of operations, and it's well fortified. Yet other options abound. A farm may work for a while, as it has food and existing

TYPES OF ZOMBIES Are we really going to break this down? You bet we are. Merging science fiction and science fact, we can draw up a list of potential methods by which zombification could happen.

BACTERIAL ZOMBIE

Perhaps a strain of bacteria that causes meningitis could mutate. This new super-bug could vandalize the brain and nervous system, until the victim was a drooling, shuffling zombie.

VIRAL ZOMBIE

A fast-acting virus could turn its victims into fast-moving monsters. Viruses are hard to treat, so this type of zombie might require a hot lead injection. I'd recommend a double dose to the cranium.

SUPERNATURAL ZOMBIE

This spooky form of the undead could be a soulless person with a pulse, or a corpse animated by otherworldly forces. Try blessed weapons, an exorcism, or a super-soaker full of holy water.

FUNGAL ZOMBIE

The fungus *Ophiocordyceps unilateralis* is also known as the "zombie fungus." *O. unilateralis* infects ants, causing them to leave the colony, bite onto a leaf, and stay there until the ant dies. This has never been seen in humans, but there's a first time for everything.

PARASITIC ZOMBIE

There are parasitic worms and other organisms that virtually hijack the brain of their host, driving them to perform suicidal acts that are part of the parasite's life cycle. The wrong worm in the wrong person could potentially make the person act like a zombie. An anti-parasite regimen could help.

DRUG ZOMBIE

The drug zombie is a very real state of self-inflicted poisoning. The drug known as "bath salts" was allegedly behind a drug-crazed "cannibal" attack in Miami in 2012, in which an assailant chewed off a man's face and plucked out both of his eyes. Police were forced to shoot the attacker five times to bring him down. Don't do drugs, kids.

RADIOLOGICAL ZOMBIE

This one's pretty far out there, since radiation normally kills things. Disagree if you like, but I find this one even less plausible than the supernatural explanation.

TECHNOLOGICAL ZOMBIE

As technology advances, so do the opportunities to meld man and machine—maybe even dead men. If the Borg tries to assimilate you, a fiery forge would incinerate circuitry and flesh.

NEUROGENESIS ZOMBIE

Neurogenesis is a process where stem cells could potentially be used to regenerate dead cells. The problem lies in the process of "reanimating" a dead person. The brain dies from the outside first. The outside is the cortex, the part that makes us who we are. The remainder of the brain, which controls basic motor function and primitive instincts, is all that's left behind. Creepy. Shoot it.

Real-Life Zombies: Fact or Fiction?

We can't ignore the thing that started the whole zombie craze, the supernatural folklore of Haiti and West Africa. In these folklore traditions, a zombie is a fresh corpse animated by magical means, such as sorcery, necromancy, or witchcraft.

While many cultures have similar folktales about scary supernatural creatures, the zombie tale has been examined seriously by at least a few experts, including the famed novelist Zora Neale Hurston.

More recently, Dr. Wade Davis, a Harvard ethnobotanist, published a paper in 1983 (followed by a popular book) suggesting that a zombie-like state could be induced by powerful mind-altering neurotoxins and psychoactive plant compounds.

The first is pufferfish toxin, which can paralyze a person. The second poison has plant compounds that can induce hallucinations and a coma-like state (often mistaken for death). Add in the oxygen deprivation and psychological trauma of being buried alive, and it sounds like a plausible recipe for a real zombie (or a least a brain-dead, living victim).

Later writers have criticized this theory, mainly because keeping someone alive, enslaved, and so heavily poisoned for years at a time would be a difficult task.

Others have suggested a cultural background has led rural people already familiar with the tradition of the zombie to misidentify homeless, mentally ill, and severely learning-disabled people as zombies, maybe even as their own deceased relatives. Whatever the real story, Haiti's zombies would seem to be part of a tradition more tragic than spooky.

CAN'T DO WITHOUT

ZOMBIE WEAPONS Weapons are the essential gear in a proposed zombie scenario. Rifles give you the option of being further away from your walking dead adversary—very smart if some pathogen was involved. But rifles can also be used at close range and for hunting the remaining wild game. Shotguns are versatile as well, due to the variety of ammunition available. Shotgun slugs can blow a big hole in a zombie. So can buckshot, and it gives you some margin for error. Handguns work too, but don't expect a zombie kill headshot with each shot fired. The brain is a relatively small target, and you'd have to be an amazing shot to nail it every time. Perhaps most iconic is some version of an entrenchment tool featuring a sturdy handle, head-bashing blade, and, in some fancy models, extra spikes and impaling tools. You never know what might work, after all.

barbed-wire fences and gates. The downside is the high visibility and the delicious-looking animals or crops. Desperate survivors will be attracted to farms, and so will non-survivors.

A stand-alone building, preferably with minimal entrances, has the potential to be a surprisingly good compound. Small high-rises, office buildings, and

T / F

THE CDC WROTE A ZOMBIE PREP GUIDE

TRUE In 2012, the Centers for Disease Control launched a campaign to inform people about the procedures and supplies needed to survive a zombie outbreak. Allegedly, their advice was meant to inspire a younger generation to consider emergency preparedness, before disaster strikes rather than after the fact. I guess their educational campaign worked, because we're still talking about it two years later. So was it a tongue-in-cheek way to inspire people to prepare for general emergencies, or does the CDC know something we don't? Only time will tell.

> IF YOU'RE BITTEN BY A ZOMBIE, DON'T LIE ABOUT IT AND HOPE IT'LL JUST CLEAR UP ON ITS OWN. IT WON'T, AND NEXT THING YOU KNOW YOU'LL BE GETTING ALL UNDEAD AND BITEY, WHICH ISN'T A GOOD LOOK FOR ANYONE.

warehouses are generally well built and offer a number of defensive possibilities. Again, your neighbors need to be onboard (if the building is a dwelling). You'll also need to shore up the first floor, because every door and window is a point of entry for the marauders and undead hordes who would try to break in.

The Achilles heel of this setup is water. You cannot rely on rainfall to provide the water for your group, and when the power goes out (which it would in a zombie uprising), there'd be no pumps running to bring water into the building. One friend of mine swears by his idea of holing up in a big-box store. No windows, lots of food and water, and all sorts of weaponry. It's certainly worth a thought, though you might have a lot of competition.

CONCEAL THE COMPOUND Staying off the radar can be one of the best defenses of all. You can do a lot to discourage nosey interlopers and prowling ghouls by using these tactics to hide your activity. Keep things quiet, both day and night.

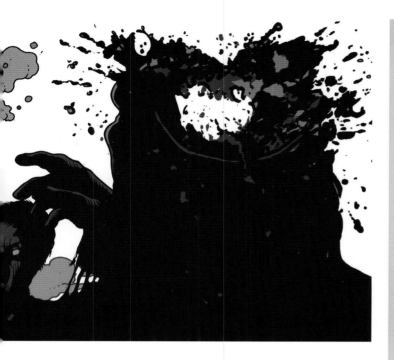

Shouting, shooting, hammering nails, and running engines and loud generators should be kept to a minimum. Keep it dark, too. When the sun goes down, you can use black trash bags or dark cloth to block off any windows that would show light coming out of a home or building. Even think of odors. The smell of cigarettes or cooking food outdoors can carry for hundreds of meters. These could alert passersby that there are desirable things to be had in your compound.

HAVE AN EXIT STRATEGY (OR TWO) In the event of a fire, a siege, or breached defenses, you'll need a way out—or better yet, several ways out. Plan these exit strategies in advance and pinpoint a handful of rendezvous spots where your group can rally if its members become separated. Consider stocking a rope ladder to get down from high points. Keep the tools handy to bust out a window on the ground floor, if needed. Make sure to seal up your fortress ahead of time so that nothing can get in—but you can still get out from several different egress points.

GOOD TO KNOW

Whatever methodology or agent created the zombies, it would be important to discover their behavior, strengths, and limitations. Consider the following traits.

SPEED The scariest movie zombies are the fast ones. The slow, plodding walkers are creepy, sure, but there's also a pathetic dopiness to them. The fast ones' speed implies some quick thinking going on in that rotting head, and that's more of a threat.

EATING HABITS Some movie franchises have focused on brain-eating undead creatures, which was explained in the films, but still made no sense. More recent incarnations of these inhumans are less finicky eaters. If people really started acting like zombies, they'd probably only have luck eating soft tissue, and be unable to open the hard skull to reach the delicious brain inside.

INDEX

ABOUT TIM MACWELCH

Tim MacWelch is the author of the *Prepare for Anything Survival Manual* and the *Hunting & Gathering Survival Manual*, and has been an active practitioner of survival and outdoor skills for over 27 years. His love of the outdoors began at a young age, growing up on a farm in Virginia, where eating wild berries, fishing, and learning about the animals of the forest were all part of country life. Tim became interested in survival skills and woodcraft as an offshoot of backpacking as a teen—while out in remote areas, it seemed like a smart plan to learn some skills. The majority of his training over the years has involved testing survival skills and devising new ones, but the biggest leaps forward came from his experience as a teacher.

Tim's teaching experiences over the years have been rich and diverse, from spending hundreds of hours volunteering to founding his year-round survival school 19 years ago. He has worked with Boy Scouts, youth groups, summer camps, and adults in all walks of life, as well as providing outdoor skills training for numerous personnel in law enforcement, search and rescue organizations, all branches of the United States Armed Forces, the State Department, and the Department of Justice and some of its agencies. Tim and his school have been featured on *Good Morning America*, several *National Geographic* programs, and in many publications including *Conde Nast Traveler*, the *Washington Post*, and *American Survival Guide*.

Since late 2010, Tim has written hundreds of pieces for *Outdoor Life* and many other publications. Tim's current and past articles and galleries can be found at outdoorlife.com and you can learn more about his survival school at www.advancedsurvivaltraining.com.

ABOUT OUTDOOR LIFE

Since it was founded in 1898, *Outdoor Life* has provided survival tips, wilderness skills, gear reports, and other essential information for hands-on outdoor enthusiasts. Each issue delivers the best advice in sportsmanship—as well as thrilling true-life tales, gear reviews, insider hunting, shooting, and fishing hints, and more—to nearly 1 million readers. Its survival-themed web site also covers disaster preparedness and the skills to thrive anywhere from the backcountry to the urban jungles.

ABOUT TIM MCDONAGH

Tim McDonagh spent his younger years growing up in a rural part of West Virginia, surrounded by rattlesnakes and snapping turtles, which in turn led to his fascination with animals. He takes a more traditional approach to illustration using brush and India ink to draw the image and then applying limited color palettes digitally. Tim now lives and works in the UK.

FROM THE AUTHOR

I'd like to dedicate this book to the survivors of every adversity, to the people with the tenacity and strength of will to survive the hardships that were placed in their path. Whether you lived through a disaster, or combat, or domestic abuse, your faith and fierce spirit allowed you to survive, even when the odds were stacked against you. Your triumph and hardiness are an example to us all. I thank you for sharing your stories and showing us that there is hope, even in the darkest of hours.

I'd also like to thank my teammates at Weldon Owen Publishing. To Mariah Bear, my editor, I thank you for the gift of your trust. I know that a book like this was on your wish list for quite a while, and a special project for you. You trusted me enough to wind me up and turn me loose on it. Thank you!

And to William Mack, thank you for your gifted design work on this book. To Bridget Fitzgerald, Ian Cannon, Katie Moore and Larry Sweazy, I thank you for your help, guidance, proofreading, brainstorming, and indexing. Last but not least, I'm very grateful for the amazing art work in this book, done by the masterful Tim McDonagh.

Thank you also to my team at *Outdoor Life* magazine. I am very appreciative for the time and input that Andrew McKean and John Taranto gave to this book. It has been a privilege to work with you again.

And thanks to the fans of the survival genre! I can't express my gratitude enough that you have matched my rabid obsession in this subject with your own ferocious interest.

-Tim MacWelch

CREDITS

ILLUSTRATIONS courtesy of **TIM MCDONAGH** (Cover, 1, 2, 20, 22, 25, 28, 33, 34, 38, 43, 52, 54, 60, 62, 65, 67, 68, 72, 80, 82, 86, 90-91, 92, 99, 100, 103, 106, 112, 117, 120, 123, 127, 129, 130, 133, 136, 139, 142, 145, 148, 154, 156, 162, 168, 170, 173, 176, 181, 184, 188, 192, 194, 198, 203, 207, 210, 215, 218, 220-221, 224 and 230-231) and **CARL WEINS** (5, 6, 7, 15, 16, 26, 31, 37, 41, 49, 50, 51, 59, 66, 71, 75, 85, 89, 95, 98, 109, 115, 118, 124, 141, 151, 159, 165, 166, 169, 179, 183, 191, 197, 201, 213 and 229)

PHOTOS courtesy of **GRIFFITH & GRIFFITH** (32), **NASA** (105), **SHUTTERSTOCK** (61, 77, 97, 111, 119, 217). All other historical images are in the public domain, authors unknown.

weldon**owen**

PRESIDENT & PUBLISHER Roger Shaw
SVP SALES & MARKETING Amy Kaneko
ASSOCIATE PUBLISHER Mariah Bear
ASSOCIATE EDITOR Ian Cannon
CREATIVE DIRECTOR Kelly Booth
ART DIRECTOR William Mack
ILLUSTRATION COORDINATOR Conor Buckley
PRODUCTION DIRECTOR Michelle Duggan
PRODUCTION MANAGER Sam Bissell
PRODUCTION DESIGNER Howie Severson
IMAGING MANAGER Don Hill

Weldon Owen would like to thank Katharine Moore for editorial help and Larry Sweazy for indexing services.

Library of Congress Control Number on file with
the publisher.

Flexi Edition: ISBN 978-1-61628-868-6
Hardcover Edition: ISBN 978-1-61628-950-8
Paperback Edition: ISBN 978-1-68188-458-5
10 9 8 7 6 5 4 3 2
2019 2020 2021 2022
Printed in China by 1010 Printing International

OUTDOORLIFE

GROUP EDITORIAL DIRECTOR Anthony Licata
GROUP MANAGING EDITOR Jean McKenna
SHOOTING EDITOR John B. Snow
DEPUTY EDITOR Gerry Bethge
MANAGING EDITOR Margaret M. Nussey
ASSISTANT EDITOR Alex Robinson
SENIOR ADMINISTRATIVE ASSISTANT Maribel Martin
GROUP CREATIVE DIRECTOR Sean Johnston
DEPUTY ART DIRECTOR Pete Sucheski
SENIOR ASSOCIATE ART DIRECTOR Kim Gray
ASSOCIATE ART DIRECTOR James A. Walsh
PHOTOGRAPHY DIRECTOR John Toolan
PRODUCTION MANAGER Judith Weber
DIGITAL DIRECTOR Nate Matthews
ONLINE CONTENT EDITOR Alex Robinson
ONLINE PRODUCER Kurt Schulitz
ASSISTANT ONLINE CONTENT EDITOR Martin Leung

2 Park Avenue
New York, NY 10016
www.outdoorlife.com